Answering Tough Interview Questions For

D0189457

Top Tips to Successful Interviewing

- Research the organisation thoroughly.
- Think about likely questions.
- Listen carefully to the question.
- Focus on what you can do for the employer.
- Give examples to illustrate your assertions.
- Talk in the first person, active tense.
- Quantify your achievements.
- Be aware of your own weak spots.
- Make sure you can explain why you want to work for the organisation.
- Prepare half a dozen questions to ask.

Being Ready for Common Questions

These questions (or at least some variation on them) come up in almost every single interview!

- *Tell us a bit about yourself.*
- *What do you know about our company?*
- *What do you think your strengths are?*
- *What would you say your weaknesses are?*
- *Why do you want to work for us?*
- *Why are you looking to leave your current job?*
- *Why should we hire you?*
- *When would you be ready to start?*
- *Where do you see yourself in five years' time?*
- *Do you have any questions for us?*

For Dummies: Bestselling Book Series for Beginners

Building Rapport with the Interviewers

- Remember to focus on both what you say and how you say it.
- Keep in mind that first impressions really do count.
- Demonstrate that you are listening to the interviewers.
- Be ready to make small talk.
- Use your body language to good effect.
- Never underestimate the power of smiling.

Pre-Interview Checklist

Before embarking on an interview, make sure that you:

- Dress to impress.
- Prepare your interview outfit the night before.
- Plan your journey to the interview.
- Pack copies of your CV.
- Rehearse your key interview responses.
- Visualise success.
- Read the morning's newspaper.
- Remember to pop in a breath mint a few minutes before your interview.

For Dummies: Bestselling Book Series for Beginners

Answering Tough Interview Questions

FOR DUMMIES®

by Rob Yeung

WILEY

Wiley Publishing, Inc.

Answering Tough Interview Questions For Dummies
Published by
John Wiley & Sons, Ltd
The Atrium
Southern Gate
Chichester
West Sussex
PO19 8SQ
England

E-mail (for orders and customer service enquires): cs-books@wiley.co.uk

Visit our Home Page on www.wileyeurope.com

Copyright © 2006 John Wiley & Sons, Ltd, Chichester, West Sussex, England

Published by John Wiley & Sons, Ltd, Chichester, West Sussex

Wiley also publishes its books in a variety of electronic formats. Some content that appears in print may not be available in electronic books.

British Library Cataloguing in Publication Data: A catalogue record for this book is available from the British Library.

ISBN-10: 0-470-01903-4 (PB)

ISBN-13: 978-0-470-01903-0 (PB)

Printed and bound in Great Britain by TJ International, Padstow, Cornwall

10 9 8 7 6 5 4 3 2 1

WILEY

About the Author

Dr Rob Yeung is a director at business psychology consultancy Talentspace, where he specialises in management assessment – training interviewers, designing assessment centres, and interviewing candidates on behalf of employers. He also tries to set aside time to coach individual job hunters on interview technique. He has interviewed candidates for jobs ranging from customer service staff to managing directors across industries as varied as banking, technology, law, accountancy, airlines, and advertising and media.

He has written for *Financial Times*, *Daily Telegraph*, and *Guardian* and contributed to publications from *Men's Health* and *New Woman* to *Accountancy* and *Sunday Times*. He has published eleven other books on career and management topics.

He is often seen on television including CNN and Channel 4's *Big Brother's Little Brother*. A chartered psychologist of the British Psychological Society with a Ph.D. in psychology from the University of London, he is a popular conference speaker and presenter of a highly acclaimed BBC television series on job hunting.

He lives with his partner in west London and can often be spotted jogging along the side of the Thames.

Dedication

To my parents – for giving me the opportunity to find my own path in life and for their eternal optimism and support. Thanks also to the Talentspace team. Especially to Steve 'Puppy' Cuthbertson for creating the space for me to get on with writing this monstrosity of a book and Ian 'Spanky' Gordon for running the business.

Author's Acknowledgements

I would like to thank Jason Dunne at Wiley for tracking me down and offering me the opportunity to write this book – I've really enjoyed it. Thanks also to Daniel Mersey for his patience with my many questions and endless changes to the shape and content of the book.

My heartfelt appreciation goes to Stuart Murphy, former controller of BBC3, and the BBC team for giving me the opportunity to work with job hunters up and down the country – and have it all filmed and broadcast to viewers on national television.

But thanks must also go to my many clients. To my corporate clients go my thanks for allowing me to introduce new interview and assessment practices into your organisations. And to the individual job hunters that I coach, my thanks go to you for constantly telling me about the appalling techniques that some of the not-so-good interviewers use!

Publisher's Acknowledgements

We're proud of this book; please send us your comments through our Dummies online registration form located at www.dummies.com/register/.

Some of the people who helped bring this book to market include the following:

Acquisitions, Editorial, and Media Development

Project Editor: Daniel Mersey

Executive Editor: Jason Dunne

Content Editor: Simon Bell

Copy Editor: Kate O'Leary

Proofreader: Andy Finch

Technical Editor: Brenda Pugh, Achieve Greatness Ltd.

Executive Project Editor: Martin Tribe

Cover Photo: © Getty Images/ Infocus International

Cartoons: Ed McLachlan

Production

Project Coordinator: Maridee Ennis

Layout and Graphics: Andrea Dahl, Stephanie Jumper, Heather Ryan, Erin Zeltner

Proofreader: Brian H. Walls

Indexer: TECHBOOKS Production Services

Publishing and Editorial for Consumer Dummies

> **Diane Graves Steele,** Vice President and Publisher, Consumer Dummies
>
> **Joyce Pepple,** Acquisitions Director, Consumer Dummies
>
> **Kristin A. Cocks,** Product Development Director, Consumer Dummies
>
> **Michael Spring,** Vice President and Publisher, Travel
>
> **Kelly Regan,** Editorial Director, Travel

Publishing for Technology Dummies

> **Andy Cummings,** Vice President and Publisher, Dummies Technology/General User

Composition Services

> **Gerry Fahey,** Vice President of Production Services
>
> **Debbie Stailey,** Director of Composition Services

Contents at a Glance

Table of Contents

Chapter 5: Talking about Problems, Perceptions, and People........................53

Chapter 6: Getting to Grips with Questions about Your Work.............................73

Chapter 7: Talking about Why You Want a New Job 89

Introduction

●●●

*C*ongratulations! In picking up *Answering Tough Interview Questions For Dummies*, you are about to embark on a journey that transforms you into the kind of high-calibre candidate who has employers fighting to hire you. Perhaps you are on the lookout for your first job or trying to return to work. Maybe you are a seasoned executive trying to climb further up the corporate ladder of success. Or perhaps you have been foxed by tough interview questions in the past and simply want to know the secret to passing them with flying colours. Whatever your situation, this book is aimed at you.

While not rocket science, interviewing can still be darned hard work. Interviewers use all manner of weird and wonderful questions and techniques designed to catch candidates out. And I should know – I've interviewed candidates on behalf of employers ranging from investment banks and insurance companies to IT companies and airlines. And I've travelled up and down the country, observing interviewers in organisations as diverse as advertising and media companies, bailiffs, funeral homes, and private detective agencies.

Although everyone can get better at interviews, you need to invest a bit of hard work in making it happen. With that in mind, I assure you that absolutely anyone can improve their interview performance by leaps and bounds by understanding the rules of the interviewing game. Enjoy working your way through this book. And good luck in your next job interview!

About This Book

In this book, I pack in everything I've discovered over the years about what interviewers want to hear, plus lessons about the most common mistakes that candidates commit and, of course, advice on how to avoid them. But I've designed this book so that you can use it as a source of reference. You don't need to read it sequentially from Chapter 1 onwards.

You may find it most useful to start with Part I, though. These chapters cover topics such as how to research a company and then, once you land an interview, how to use your body language and tone of voice to make the best possible impact with what you actually talk about. I recommend that you at least skim through Chapter 2 on how to research a company, because probably the most important factor in succeeding at interviews is to tailor all your answers to what each particular set of interviewers is looking for.

Conventions Used in This Book

To help you navigate through this book, pay attention to a few conventions:

- *Italic* is used to emphasise important words and highlight new words and terms that you may not have come across before; italic is also used for direct speech – either questions from the interviewer or answers you may want to give.

- **Boldface** is used to point out key terms in numbered steps and bulleted lists.

- `Monofont` is used for occasional Web addresses, which direct you to further sources of information.

Foolish Assumptions

In this book, I have made some assumptions about you:

- You want to improve on your interview performance in order to win over interviewers and secure a job. Perhaps you've been knocked back from a couple of interviews already or you have found interviews difficult in the past. Or maybe you just know that interviewers are getting more and more picky and asking increasingly difficult questions.

- You want bite-sized pieces of advice that explain what you need to say in order to impress an interviewer, along with examples to illustrate how to put that advice into practice in formulating a response.

✔ You will read the example answers but are willing to put some effort into devising your own. After all, you may be a first-time job hunter or a seasoned executive looking for one last job before retirement, so the answers in this book cannot possibly apply to everyone.

How This Book Is Organised

This book is organised into five major parts. The chapters within each part cover specific topic areas in more detail. And each chapter is further subdivided into sections relating to particular topics. In addition, a detailed Table of Contents at the beginning of the book helps you navigate around. I've used this layout to help you to go straight to the topics that are of most interest to you.

Part 1: Making Sure You Shine in an Interview

A lot of what determines success in an interview depends on doing some research and preparation. In this part, I tell you about the key skills and qualities that pretty much all interviewers are looking for. I also talk you through how to research an organisation to understand how to pitch your answers at the right level. And I explain how to build chemistry with the interviewers to ensure that they not only respect your skills and experience, but also like the person that you are.

Part 11: Answering Tough Interview Questions

Interviewers tend to recycle the same questions from one interview to the next. In this part, I tell you about the most common questions that interviewers like to ask. I share insider tips with you on how to tell the interviewers what they want to hear so you can win them over.

Part III: Dealing with Tricky Questions and Other Situations

This part takes you through the many questions and devious techniques that interviewers can use to take the right candidate to the next level. I explain how to handle questions aimed at everyone from school leavers and graduates to women returning from maternity and candidates who have been made redundant. I also tell you how to deal with situations ranging from being asked illegal questions to assessment centres and being interviewed over the phone.

Part IV: Securing the Job of Your Dreams

This part takes you through the secrets to rounding off the perfect interview. I describe how to think up the perfect questions to ask the interviewers and how to make a great impression on the interviewers as you leave. Finally, I explain how to follow up the feedback from an interview to have the best possible chance of getting the job.

Part V: The Part of Tens

This part is a *For Dummies* favourite. Here, I guide you through the ten commonest mistakes that candidates make and list my top ten hints for having a satisfying and fulfilling career. Enjoy!

Icons Used in This Book

To help you, all *For Dummies* books lay out key points of advice in an easy-to-use format. Look out for these icons throughout the book:

This icon points to useful ideas that help you to improve your interview performance.

This icon highlights key information that you must bear in mind in order to impress the interviewers.

As you may have guessed, this icon is reserved for the bits of advice that you really, really need to take on board. Look out for these alerts and ignore them at your peril – it can cost you a job!

This icon highlights technical stuff that you don't necessarily need to understand. If pushed for time, you can simply skip over these. However, I have included them just in case you want to understand a bit more about the theory behind inter-viewers' questions and techniques.

Where to Go from Here

This book is written so that you can jump to whatever topic most interests you. If, for example, you are trying to appear calmer and more confident in interviews, then make Chapter 3 your first port of call. If you need to prepare for competency-based interviews, then go straight to Chapter 9. Or if you want to find out more about explaining a change of career direction, then skip ahead to Chapter 11. Don't feel the need to stand on ceremony – feel free to skip ahead to the topics that grab your interest.

Whatever you decide to read first, remember that this book is packed with examples of how other people may answer tough interview questions. Make sure that you read the advice and devise your own answer to the question – otherwise a canny interviewer will see straight through you.

Part I

Making Sure You Shine in an Interview

"And what makes you think you will be suited to a sales position with this company, Mr. Bucktrellis?"

In this part . . .

1 f you want to start out on the journey of getting ready to face anything that interviewers can throw at you, this is the part for you.

Interviews are a game. And in any game, rules exist. So in this part I talk about the most essential rules of succeeding in tough interviews. First, you need to find out how to win the game. What are interviewers looking for? Whether going for a job as a senior manager or an office junior, employers are looking for a core set of skills and characteristics. So make sure that you demonstrate those skills and qualities. The second rule of the game is to do your research and preparation. Do it and succeed; don't do it and fail – it's as simple as that. The third rule is to think about not only what you say but also how you say it. Interviewers are not just looking for bright and committed people – they want people who can visibly appear enthusiastic and motivated too.

Chapter 1

Understanding the Interviewing Game

*T*he job market is increasingly competitive, and many interviewers are inundated with too many applications. In this chapter, I share with you the secrets of what interviewers are really looking for, and how to prepare the ammunition for your answers.

This book contains plenty of advice and loads of mock answers to tough interview questions. But simply reading through the book won't get you anywhere. What you need to do is figure out how *you* would answer different interview questions by using my answers for inspiration.

Recognising What Interviewers Are Looking For

At first glance, different job adverts seem to be looking for a dazzling array of skills, experience, and qualities. But in actuality, most employers are really looking for three basic factors for finding the right person for the job. These three factors can be summarised as *the three Cs* of interviews:

- **Competence:** Interviewers look to recruit people who have the skills and personal qualities to do the job with minimal supervision.

- **Commitment:** Interviewers want to give the job to someone who sticks at it. They want a self-motivated person who persists in the face of difficulties rather than gives up at the first sign of trouble.

- **Chemistry:** Interviewers want someone that they feel they can get on with. All employers feel they have a unique culture – and want to know that you can fit in with the rest of the team.

Demonstrate your competence and commitment by giving good answers to the many questions thrown at you. You can only create chemistry by using your tone of voice and body language to demonstrate that you are the kind of likeable person who gets on with everyone. Be aware that the interviewers are not only evaluating *what* you say, but also *how* you say it. No matter what section of the book you turn to, be sure to keep the 'three Cs' in mind.

Finding Out about Key Skills and Qualities

When interviewers say they're looking for 'competent' candidates, what exactly do they mean? Well, dozens of surveys have asked employers what they want from potential recruits. This section covers the top ten skills and personal qualities that employers look for. Parts II and III take you through how to answer these questions, but for now, make a mental note of these skills and then weigh up whether you possess them.

Interestingly, most of the surveys agree that these skills and characteristics tend to apply to employees at all levels of an organisation and across most industry sectors. So a high-street retailer looking for a shop assistant tends to want more or less the same skills and qualities as an international corporation looking for a senior manager – although obviously to differing degrees.

Communicating with people

Unless you are being hired to work in a sealed room with no contact with colleagues or customers (which I very much doubt!), you need to have good communication skills.

When discussing your communication skills with interviewers, think of examples of occasions when you:

 ✔ Listened to the needs of other people, such as colleagues or customers.

 ✔ Conveyed information to other people – perhaps on a one-to-one basis or to a group of people.

 ✔ Handled difficult situations, such as customer complaints, on the telephone.

 ✔ Used your written communication skills in preparing reports or documents for other people to read.

See Chapter 3 for more about communication skills.

Influencing others

Although communication skills are important, most employers want people who also have powers of persuasion – being able to win others over or change their minds. In preparing for your interviews, think of times when you have

 ✔ Had a discussion with someone and helped him or her to see your point of view.

 ✔ Changed someone's mind.

 ✔ Persuaded someone to take a course of action that they were initially not in support of.

Persuasion skills are particularly prized when dealing with customers or clients – for example, in listening to their needs and then selling products or services to them.

See Chapters 4, 5, and 9 for more on influencing skills.

Analysing situations

Managers want to hire candidates who can research issues and assess situations. Make sure that you think about times when you:

✔ Gathered information about a topic or issue.

✔ Broke down a complex problem into a number of smaller issues.

✔ Weighed up the pros and cons of different options.

See Chapters 9 and 12 for more about analytical skills.

Solving problems

Employers are looking for people who can assess situations and then work out the best course of action to take. Be ready to talk to interviewers about occasions when you:

✔ Made suggestions about how to tackle a problem.

✔ Initiated or participated in brainstorming sessions.

✔ Took a course of action to solve a problem or tackle an issue.

See Chapters 9 and 12 for more about problem-solving skills.

Demonstrating drive and determination

Organisations do not want to hire people who only work when given explicit instructions as to what to do; they want to hire candidates who are self-motivated and can demonstrate a bit of initiative. Think back to times when you:

> ✔ Suffered a setback or disappointment at work but got back on your feet and got on with a task.
>
> ✔ Had an original idea and used it to be more effective or productive at work.
>
> ✔ Overcame a difficulty or obstacle that was preventing you from achieving a goal.

Chapters 4, 5, and 9 contain more information on demonstrating drive and determination.

Teamworking with colleagues

Employers are constantly talking about the need for employees to work together more effectively as a team. Try to recall instances when you:

> ✔ Helped someone else in the team with their work or duties.
>
> ✔ Resolved conflict or disagreement between other team members.
>
> ✔ Provided a team member with a shoulder to cry on.

Effective teamworking is about putting the needs of the team above those of your own.

Chapters 5, 9, and 12 contain some examples of popular questions about teamworking.

Developing quickly

Especially for entry-level jobs (including graduate entry roles), employers want people who can develop quickly in the job. Managers don't want to hire people who need a lot of handholding! In preparing for interviews, try to think back to times when you:

> ✔ Became proficient at a task or duty more quickly than others expected.
>
> ✔ Gained knowledge about a topic or issue because of your hard work and dedication.
>
> ✔ Picked up a new skill with minimal supervision.

See Chapters 4, 6, and 9 for questions relating to your ability to pick up new skills and absorb information quickly.

Being flexible and adaptable

Employers want to hire people who are open-minded, accommodating, and willing to help out when the need arises. Try to recall occasions when you:

- Offered to do overtime to help get a project or piece of work completed on time.
- Helped someone else even when it was not part of your job description.
- Changed your mind at work after listening to someone else's point of view.

Chapters 5 and 9 show examples of questions about how you may have demonstrated your flexibility and adaptability in different work situations.

Planning and organising

Employers are always on the lookout for candidates who can manage their own workload. In order to convince employers that you possess these skills, think about instances when you:

- Prioritised tasks to meet a tough deadline.
- Planned out and then completed a project.
- Organised other people to ensure that a piece of work got done.

Chapter 9 contains examples of typical questions about pieces of work you may have planned.

Being aware of the bigger picture

Employers complain that a lot of employees have a very narrow-minded view of their work. They don't see the 'bigger picture' of what goes on outside of their team, department, or organisation. Demonstrate that you are aware of the bigger picture by thinking back to occasions when you:

- ✔ Had to liaise with colleagues outside of your department.
- ✔ Found out some interesting information about a customer, supplier, or competitor and then shared it with colleagues.
- ✔ Thought about the impact of your work or duties on people outside of your own team.

Chapters 2 and 7 give advice on demonstrating your awareness of the bigger picture.

Getting invited to interviews

The majority of this book covers how to cope with the many questions asked by interviewers. But if you're not getting invited to interviews in the first place, you may want to consider some of these tips:

✔ **Revise your CV:** Avoid sending exactly the same CV to every single job that you go for. Most people tailor their covering letter, but for extra points tailor your CV to each individual application as well. If, for example, you are applying for a customer service job, make sure you draw out your experience with customers.

✔ **Get a second opinion:** Ask a friend or trusted colleague to comment on your CV and covering letters. Their objectivity may allow them to spot errors that you make in your job applications.

✔ **Gain more of the right experience:** If you have made every effort to revise your CV and tailor your covering letter, perhaps you lack the right experience and skills. You may need to rethink the kind of jobs that you are applying for.

Chapter 2

Doing Your Job Interview Homework

Congratulations if you're being invited to attend an interview. Most employers receive dozens or even hundreds of applications for every job – so being invited to an interview means you've already beaten off a large chunk of the competition.

However, many candidates go wrong by turning up for the interview without doing any research about the company and preparation for the interview. In this chapter, I tell you exactly how you can research and prepare to give a great interview performance.

Researching the Company

Interviewers want more than a candidate with just the right skills and experience – they want to hire someone who desires working for their particular organisation. And the way to demonstrate that you are keen is to research the company thoroughly so that you can talk confidently about it.

Gathering vital information

Begin your research by reading any information that an organisation sends you – for example, recruitment brochures, prospectuses, job descriptions, and even catalogues of their products or services.

Even if an organisation doesn't send you any information, look at their Web site. If you can't find their site on the Internet, try calling the organisation to ask for the Web address.

Good research can make the difference between success and failure. Make sure that you spend at least a couple of hours reading the organisation's literature and scouring their Web site for information.

Absorb as much information as you can about the company, their aims and objectives, and what they do. At a very minimum, find the answers to questions such as:

- ✔ What are the goals or objectives of the organisation?

- ✔ How many people work for the organisation?

- ✔ Where is the organisation based? Do they operate only within the UK, or in Europe, or globally?

- ✔ Where is their main office or corporate headquarters? How many offices, shops, or branches does the organisation have?

- ✔ What are the organisation's main services or products?

Collecting in-depth information

To find out even more about an organisation, try typing their name into an Internet search engine to see what else you can come up with. Look for information regarding the following list of questions:

- ✔ When was the company founded? Who were the founders? (This is a particularly important question for smaller organisations.)

- ✔ What is the name of the organisation's chief executive officer (CEO) or managing director?

- ✔ Who are the organisation's main competitors? How does this particular organisation differ from its competitors?

- ✔ What major threats and issues affect the organisation?

- ✔ Is the company growing and expanding? If so, what are its stated goals and priorities with regards to growth?

- ✔ How is the organisation performing financially?

Visiting shops and premises

If an organisation has shops, branches, showrooms, or other properties open to the public, visit at least one of them. Even better, try to visit a couple of their premises to get a feel for how the organisation likes to present itself to the public.

Visiting an organisation's premises is particularly important if applying for a job with a retailer. Retail employers often ask candidates what they do and don't like about their shops. If you don't make the effort to visit one of their stores, you may be rejected for not demonstrating enough interest in the company.

Preparing Answers to Common Questions

If you do your research beforehand, you'll have great answers to lots of the questions posed by your interviewers.

The secret to predicting likely topics of discussion during an interview is scrutinising the original advertisement that drew your attention to the job. Always keep a copy of every job advert you apply for so that you can refer to it if invited to attend an interview.

Linking job adverts to key skills

This section shows examples of job adverts and how to identify the key skills, experience, and qualities that you may need to talk about during an interview.

Take a look at the job advert for an office manager that's shown in Figure 2-1. The key words and phrases show questions that interviewers are almost certain to ask candidates applying for this job:

- ✔ **'Experienced office manager':** This phrase tells you that the interviewers will want to know how long you've worked as an office manager.

- ✔ **'Excellent written and oral communication':** Be prepared to give examples of documents that you've written. And, be ready to talk about how you communicate with people both in person and on the telephone.

✔ **'Lead a team of four':** Have you led a team in the past? Can you talk about your style of leadership? Be able to give examples of how you built your team, delegated to them, and disciplined them.

✔ **'Supporting':** Make sure that you can talk about how you have supported other people in doing their jobs.

Job advert 1: Office Manager

We are looking for an experienced office manager to help us run our office. You must have excellent written and oral communication skills. You will lead a team of four administrative assistants in supporting a total office of 20 people. In return, we offer a competitive salary for the right individual.

Figure 2-1: Job advert for an office manager.

As you can see, you can quite quickly predict many of the questions that the interviewers are likely to ask you. Here's the breakdown of key words and phrases used in the job advert for a sales position, shown in Figure 2-2.

✔ **'Self-motivated':** Of course, the interviewers may ask you whether you would describe yourself as self-motivated. But can you give any examples of how you have motivated yourself to achieve goals?

✔ **'High-street retailer':** Do you have any retail or customer experience that you can talk about? If not, be ready to talk about why you want to work in retail.

✔ **'Flexible and willing to work shift patterns':** If you have worked shifts in the past, make sure that you mention this. If you haven't worked shifts before, think about some of the difficulties doing so may pose for you – and how you can overcome them.

- **'Outgoing personality':** How will you convince the interviewers that you have an outgoing personality? You need to inject plenty of energy into your interview performance, but also think about stories to illustrate how you enjoy spending time with people.

- **'Build a career in retail':** This phrase implies that the interviewers are looking for someone who wants to join their company and stay for a number of years rather than someone who sees working in the store as a temporary position. So be ready for questions such as: *What are your longer-term career plans?*

Job advert 2: Sales Advisor

Self-motivated people required! We are looking for sales advisors for a busy high-street retailer. Successful candidates must be flexible and willing to work shift patterns. You should have an outgoing personality and be looking to build a career in retail. Good hourly rates.

Figure 2-2: Job advert for a sales advisor.

Consider these key words and phrases when preparing to go for an executive position, such as the job advertised in Figure 2-3:

- **'Working with the sales team':** Prepare to talk about the trials and tribulations of working with sales people. If you haven't worked with sales teams before, then be prepared to explain how you'll go about working with them.

- **'Writing marketing materials':** Do you have examples of marketing material that you can talk about?

- **'Managing our Web site':** Can you talk about how you have updated another organisation's Web site or at least contributed to one in the past? Are you ready to talk about using software to manage this company's Web site?

- **'Dealing with newspapers and trade journals':** Be ready to talk about how you have dealt with journalists in the past. What success stories can you share for how you have promoted a previous employer through working with journalists?

✔ **'Ambitious':** How will you prove to the interviewers that you're ambitious? What major achievements can you cite to demonstrate your ambition?

✔ **'Experience in the IT sector':** Be prepared to talk about other IT companies that you've worked for.

Job advert 3: Marketing Executive

As a fast-growing software company, we are looking to expand our team by recruiting an experienced marketing executive. Responsibilities include: working with the sales team; writing marketing materials including brochures and press releases; managing our Web site; and dealing with newspapers and trade journals. We are looking for an ambitious professional with experience in the IT sector. Contact Laura Hall in confidence for more information on 020 8700 1234.

Figure 2-3: Job advert for a marketing executive.

Dressing for Success

Making snap judgements about people is human nature, and a lot of interviewers believe that a candidate's dress code says a lot about him or her. Make the right impression on the interviewers by thinking carefully about what to wear on the big day.

Not that long ago, interviewers expected all candidates to turn up in suits. Now, an increasing number of organisations have relaxed their dress codes, and it has become impossible to prescribe how to dress for just about any interview.

 Always call ahead and ask about the dress code. Or, if you are at all uncertain, then go on a scouting trip and watch the flow of people as they go in and out of the building where you are to be interviewed. However, even if the majority of the staff seem to dress casually, do be careful as many interviewers may dress smartly specifically for interviews.

 Wearing a suit may not always be your best option. For example, people in creative roles in industries such as fashion, advertising, and media often talk scathingly about *suits* – people in (what they see as) boring roles such as finance, operations, and human resources. No matter what, be sure to think about your clothes.

'Getting' the default for men

If in doubt, go smart. Being slightly overdressed is always better than being underdressed (you can always take off your tie and undo a top button). For men, this means the following:

- ✔ **Wear a dark suit:** Navy blue and grey are the most acceptable colours. Black can come across as a bit funereal. And buy a classic cut with a two- or three-button jacket rather than trying to follow the latest fashion.

- ✔ **Wear a plain, long-sleeved shirt:** Pick a pale colour such as light blue or white. If you suffer from sweating, then wear a white t-shirt underneath to prevent wet patches from showing.

- ✔ **Wear a plain silk tie:** Patterns can be distracting. Let your words rather than your tie entertain the interviewers.

- ✔ **Wear black shoes:** Opt for plain lace-ups without fancy buckles. Polish your shoes. One school of thought amongst interviewers says that unpolished shoes are the sign of a disorganised mind.

Understanding the guidelines for women

As for men (see the preceding section), if in doubt, go smart. But women's rules are less rigid, because so many more options are available. However, here are some guidelines if you're unsure about the dress code:

✔ **Wear a neutral or dark-coloured suit:** For interviews with a professional services firm or a big business, wear a suit as opposed to separates. And think carefully before opting for a trouser suit, as a few older, male interviewers are still a bit sexist about women in trousers as opposed to skirts.

✔ **Wear a plain top:** Choose an unpatterned blouse or fitted top in a pale colour. Avoid sleeveless tops and don't go for anything too sexy.

✔ **Keep jewellery to a minimum:** Wear only one pair of earrings and a maximum of one ring on each hand. Avoid thumb rings or too many bangles as they may distract from a professional appearance.

Getting Ready to Go

Before you set off, here are a few final thoughts for you in the days before the interview:

✔ **Know the time, date, and location of the interview:** You also need to work out the precise route to get there. If in any doubt as to how long the journey takes, add extra time. Being late is an unforgivable sin.

✔ **Know the format for the interview:** How many interviewers will attend the interview? Is there just one interview, several interviews, or a mixture of interviews and psychometric tests? If you don't know, find out by ringing up the human resources department, the recruitment coordinator, or perhaps an interviewer's personal assistant.

✔ **Have copies of your CV to hand:** Because CVs can go astray, print out a half-dozen copies of your CV and be prepared to give them to interviewers who may not have a copy. Carry the copies of your CV in a briefcase or a plain folder.

✔ **Take a newspaper or business magazine:** If you arrive more than half an hour before the interview, find a local cafe rather than sitting in the interviewers' reception – being too early can signal over-anxiousness.

Preparing your CV

The majority of British employers ask to see your *CV* (or *curriculum vitae*). A CV is a two or three page summary of your skills and experience.

Make sure that your CV reflects the kinds of words and phrases that the job advert uses. For example, if the ad talks about 'planning' and 'dealing with customers', make sure that you use those precise words if you possibly can.

Include the following details in your CV:

✔ Your contact details including your name, address, contact telephone numbers, and email address.

✔ A list of your experience in *reverse chronological order* (starting at the top of the list with your most recent job and working backwards in time)

✔ Your education, including any professional qualifications. But don't list out the exams you took at school if you left school more than ten years ago.

✔ Any relevant hobbies or interests – but be sure to explain why they are relevant.

If you're not sure about how to set out your CV, take a look at Steve Shipside and Joyce Lain Kennedy's *CVs For Dummies* (Wiley).

Nerves can make you sweat and cause your mouth to go dry. Your body odour can become pronounced and your breath may be unpleasant! Deodorise thoroughly on the big day and pop in a couple of breath mints in the minutes before an interview to make sure that the interviewers don't remember you for entirely the wrong reasons.

Chapter 3

Polishing Your Interview Performance

*I*magine the scenario: Two candidates both say, *I'm the right person for the job because I have good people skills*. But imagine one candidate mumbling the words in a lifeless fashion, avoiding eye contact, and fidgeting nervously, while a second candidate says the words in a dynamic fashion, smiling and looking eye-to-eye at the interviewers. Who do you think the interviewers are going to give the job to?

Your body language and tone of voice have important roles to play in convincing the interviewers that you're the best candidate. In this chapter, I talk about ways to make sure that you grab the attention of the interviewers.

Creating the Right Impact

You probably won't be surprised when I tell you that interviewers are looking to recruit motivated and enthusiastic people. But you may be surprised to discover that most of your interpersonal impact comes across not in *what* you say, but *how* you say it.

Research claims that up to 55 per cent of our communication effectiveness is determined by our body language, comprising of our gestures, movements, and facial expressions.

A lot of candidates talk about trying to 'be themselves' during interviews. These candidates say that they tend to warm up only when they get to know people better and that they feel fake in having to 'act up' with interviewers. But remember that interviews are a game of sorts: Interviewers want to hire candidates who are energetic and enthusiastic from the moment they meet, so you need to focus on performing as a dynamic and passionate person – even if that isn't how you normally like to behave until you know people better.

Making eye contact

Eye contact is critical in interviews. Failing to look the interviewers in the eye conveys an impression of nervousness – or that you are embellishing on the truth. Assuming that you don't want to be perceived as anxious or a fraudster, you must develop the skill of making solid eye contact.

However, good eye contact doesn't mean staring at the interviewers throughout your conversation with them. In fact, two rules govern eye contact:

- ✔ Look when the interviewers talk: Aim to look at an interviewer for at least 90 per cent of the time when he or she is asking questions or otherwise speaking.

- ✔ Look away for part of the time when you talk: Looking away is okay for a portion of the time when speaking. For example, a lot of candidates tend to look away for a few seconds when they are trying to recall an example. Making more than 90 per cent eye contact when you are speaking will probably freak the interviewers out! Aim to look at them for around a half to two-thirds of the time when you are speaking.

Use *active listening* to demonstrate that you are listening to the interviewers. This means nodding occasionally as they speak and using words and phrases such as *yes*, *uh-huh*, and *I understand* occasionally to signal that you follow what they are saying.

Using your body language

You can tell a huge amount about what goes on inside a person's head by how they use their body language. For example, playing with a ring or repeatedly touching your hair are often interpreted as signs of nervousness. A slouched posture or drumming fingers on a table can be construed as a lack of interest. Follow these tips to project the right kind of image:

- **Stand and sit up straight:** Lengthen your body and hold your spine erect. Maintain a straight posture during an interview. Don't let tiredness or nerves allow your shoulders to hunch forwards.

- **Stop any fidgeting:** Don't give away any hint of nerves by moving around in a restless fashion. Keep your hands clasped lightly in your lap or rest them gently on the table.

- **Use your hands to emphasise key points:** Hand gestures can make people seem more sincere or credible. So use your hands occasionally to underscore key points to make yourself visually more engaging – for example, by turning your palms up and spreading your fingers to indicate sincerity or counting points off on your fingers.

- **Avoid crossing your arms:** Some interviewers read crossing your arms as being a sign of defensiveness. So don't do it. However, contrary to popular opinion, you *can* cross your legs – so long as you don't cross your arms across your chest as well.

- **Keep your legs still:** Avoid crossing or uncrossing your legs or tapping your feet. Such fidgeting can be unnerving.

Use your hands to emphasise key points only when you are speaking. Keep your hands still when the interviewers are speaking to show that you're listening.

Avoid pointing at the interviewers – this aggressive gesture can seem intimidating.

Creating warmth by smiling

Don't tell anyone, but here's a little secret: Interviewers often hire the candidate that they *like* the most rather than picking the most skilled and experienced person for the job. All interviewers are subconsciously affected by factors such as warmth, rapport, and smiling.

Now, too much smiling makes you come across as a manic Cheshire cat. Following these hints generates an impression of warmth and likeability rather than an unhinged personality:

✔ **Smile as you greet the interviewers:** First impressions really count. So make sure that you are positively beaming when you first meet the interviewers. Project the impression that you are incredibly pleased to be at the interview.

✔ **Smile when you talk about your strengths or achievements:** Smiling would be incongruous when talking about difficult situations at work. But if talking about positive aspects of yourself and your working life, try to add a smile at some point.

✔ **Smile when you leave the room:** When you say your goodbyes and thank the interviewers for their time, give them another broad smile to show that you enjoyed meeting them.

Common vocal mistakes

Job candidates tend to make one of three mistakes when it comes to their voice during an interview. They often:

✔ **Speak in a monotonous voice:** The words seem to fall out of these candidates' mouths without any energy or inflection behind them.

✔ **Mumble words:** The lips of these candidates simply don't move enough to let the interviewers understand what they're trying to say. Unfortunately, interviewers are usually too polite to say that they can't understand you and simply let you mumble on. But you can be certain that they'll give the job to someone that they can understand!

✔ **Speak too quickly or for too long:** Nerves can get the better of some candidates and make them gibber almost uncontrollably or speak for too long. Speak for no more than one or two minutes at a time. If you want to continue a story, check with the interviewers by asking, *Is this useful, shall I go on?*

Using intonation and inflection

Interviewers can spend a couple of days at a time interviewing. And they can feel really bored when all candidates seem to be saying pretty much the same thing. To make the interviewers sit up and take notice of what you're saying, focus on your tone of voice.

Follow these guidelines to come across as an interesting and enthusiastic – but also calm and confident – candidate:

- ✔ **Introduce inflection into your speech:** Actors sometimes talk of using 'light and shade' in a voice. Occasionally raise the tone of your voice or speed up the pace to convey excitement or passion about a topic. Deepen your voice or slow down a little to transmit seriousness.

- ✔ **Emphasise key words:** Say key words and phrases a little louder to make them stand out. This tactic is the auditory equivalent of typing important words in a **bold** typeface.

- ✔ **Articulate your words carefully:** If in any doubt as to whether you pronounce your words clearly enough, ask a variety of colleagues for their opinion. Don't ask friends, as they are too used to your way of speaking to give you objective feedback.

- ✔ **Think about leaving pauses between sentences:** Remember that full stops appear at the end of sentences. Make sure not to let your sentences all run together.

Intonation and inflection are really difficult to get right. The best way to tell if you sound okay is to tape record yourself saying interview answers out loud and then listen to your responses to see how they come across.

Rehearsing for the big day

To pull off a cracking interview, keep in mind the 'three Ps' of interviewing:

- ✔ Preparation

- ✔ Practice

- ✔ Performance

Saying interview answers out loud can make an enormous difference to your confidence in an actual interview. To observe your body language and expressions, try saying your answers out loud in front of a mirror.

Building Your Confidence

A lot of candidates find interviews nerve-wracking. Many of
them are otherwise calm, cool, and collected individuals, but
find that something about interviews just sets them off and
makes them feel edgy and unable to present themselves at
their best.

Feeling nervous at interviews can create a vicious cycle. You
feel nervous, which makes you perform badly at interviews.
But the fact that you perform badly at interviews understandably makes you feel nervous. For advice on feeling more confident, consult Romilla Ready and Kate Burton's *Neuro-linguistic
Programming For Dummies*, and Kate Burton and Brinley Platt's
Building Confidence For Dummies (both published by Wiley).

Getting Off to a Great Start

You may have heard people say that most interviewers make
up their minds within the first five to ten minutes of an interview. And, in many cases, it's true – a lot of interviewers judge
candidates on what they say and do within those initial few
minutes.

So make sure that you put in a commanding performance:

- Offer a solid handshake.
- Demonstrate your enthusiasm.
- Make a positive comment.
- Be prepared for some chitchat.
- Wait until the interviewers indicate for you to sit.

Concentrate on making a great impression in those first few
minutes and the interviewers may well warm to you and make
the rest of the interview that much more enjoyable. But keep
your guard up at all times – listen carefully to every question,
never interrupt the interviewers, and think before you speak!

Part II
Answering Tough Interview Questions

"That's a strange leisure interest you've got, Miss Muddlestone – hypnotism."

In this part . . .

*T*his part covers the questions – both ordinary and extreme – that interviewers can and do use to find out more about you.

I cover all the common questions you may be asked in interviews. Interviewers almost certainly want to know about your skills and experience, your career history, and why you want a new job. They may also want to hear about your people skills and review your schooling and education. Some interviewers use a special technique called competency-based interviewing, while others prefer the more dubious tactics of pressure interviewing – trying to catch you off guard with the aim of glimpsing the 'real' you. In this part, I explain what the interviewers are looking for and help you to construct your own interview responses.

Chapter 4

Talking about Yourself

In This Chapter

▶ Thriving on the questions that interviewers love to ask

▶ Covering essential work skills

*I*n interviewing – as in life – there is both good news and bad. Interviewers tend to be a fairly lazy breed, which means that they often end up recycling the same old questions for interview after interview. For you, that's good news because it means that most interviewers end up asking more or less the same questions as each other.

But the bad news is that you can't simply find out the right answers to give from a book. Sure, I'm going to give you lots of examples to illustrate the right sorts of key words and phrases to use. But at the end of the day, make sure that your answers reflect your personality, your skills, and your experience. You need to find ways to stand out from the crowd. So a great answer for an 18-year-old school leaver looking for their first job may be a tad different from what may work for a seasoned 50-year-old executive!

Handling General Questions about Yourself

Let's start with the ten most popular questions asked by interviewers. Giving comfortable responses to commonly asked interview questions is a foot in the door for any candidate. If you go to an interview and the interviewer doesn't ask you at least a few of these gems, well, I'll be amazed!

Driving toward great examples

Brrm brrm. The acronym CAR helps you to construct great examples to back up your claims that you are as good as you say you are. Whenever possible, try to explain the following points in your examples:

- **Challenge:** What was the problem or opportunity you had to tackle? Set the scene for the story that you are about to tell – but try to do it in only two or three sentences.

- **Actions:** What actions did you take to resolve the problem or grasp the opportunity? This is the bulk of your story. Use the first person singular ('I') rather than the first person plural ('we') to describe the actions that you took.

- **Result:** What was the outcome of the actions that you took?

Generally, try to choose examples that describe successful outcomes.

Coming up with different examples for every skill that you may need to talk about in an interview can be really difficult. So you may end up using a handful of examples to demonstrate multiple skills. For instance, if you were involved in negotiating a deal with a customer, you may have demonstrated skills including researching the customer, writing a presentation, giving the presentation, putting together a business plan, and so on. You can get away with referring back to the same example to illustrate different skills, but each time you do it, don't bore the interviewer by going through all the CAR acronym. Just focus on the actions that you took to demonstrate that particular skill.

Anyone can claim that they are a fantastic leader, a superb problem-solver, a go-getting team player, and an all-round good egg. But just as a lawyer in court needs to cite evidence to substantiate an argument, you need to provide examples to justify your claims. So as you read through the following questions, come up with your own personal example for each answer.

Tell me about yourself

This is probably the single most popular question that interviewers use for opening an interview. But don't take the question as an invitation to recount your entire life's history. When you hear this question, answer by pretending that they had actually asked you: *Tell me **briefly** about your professional experience and the relevant qualities that make you a strong candidate for this job.*

Don't make the classic mistake of sharing too much personal information with your interviewer. I've heard too many candidates start by telling the interviewer where they were born and where they went to school and what they studied there. It's not a wrong answer as such, but by telling them about your personal history, your opportunity to sell your experience and relevant skills flies by.

All the interviewer needs is a snapshot – a summary lasting no more than a minute or 90 seconds – of your background and experience. Be sure to prepare one before your interview.

Read the original job advertisement and pick up on the key words and phrases the interviewers are looking for. These may be about certain skills or experience, or perhaps human qualities they want the perfect candidate to have. Squeeze some of these words and phrases into your answer. For instance, if the advert mentions that the employer is looking for 'a supervisor with excellent communication and people management skills', mention any supervisory experience you've gained, as well as the fact that you are articulate and enjoy communicating and liaising with a wide range of people.

Example answers include:

> ✔ *I am a management consultant with 12 years' experience gained across industries and sectors ranging from financial services and retail to petrochemicals and media. I am responsible for business development activities and last year sold projects totalling £400,000 to clients. On a day-to-day basis, I also manage a team of up to eight consultants and junior consultants. But more than being a good consultant, I like to think of myself as a fair and democratic person as I try hard to listen to my clients as well as my team.*

> ✔ *I'm currently the floor supervisor at Molly's, which is a busy bar and restaurant in Brighton. I'm responsible for all aspects of management, ranging from stock taking and ordering to end of day cashing up. I run a team of seven staff and am responsible for training, hiring, and firing. The hours can be quite long, but I enjoy it and like the mix of activities from dealing with customers to managing the staff.*

✔ *I've been a childcare assistant for the last three years, working with physically and mentally impaired children between the ages of eight and 14. I've really enjoyed it and have developed some skills such as being creative and being extremely patient. I also spend a lot of time dealing with the children's parents and have to demonstrate really good listening skills with them. I've now decided that I want to expand my horizons and travel, which is why I've decided to change careers into being a holiday rep – but I hope that my creativity, patience, and listening skills will hold me in good stead in this new industry.*

What are your strengths?

From your analysis of the job advert (refer to Chapter 2), you can work out the key skills and characteristics that the employer is looking for. Paraphrasing a few of these back to the employer is an effective way to answer this question.

When paraphrasing key skills and characteristics, make sure to change the wording slightly – simply repeating them verbatim will make you sound like a mindless parrot.

A couple of examples:

✔ *As an office manager with Global Gadgets, I have excellent organisation skills and really good attention to detail – I'm not the sort of person who does things by halves. I also believe that I have good communication skills in dealing with not only external customers but also all members of the internal team – from the senior managers to the junior researchers.*

✔ *I've been told that I'm a very good manager. My team tells me that I give them a lot of freedom in how to do their work, which they really appreciate. They also say that I'm really enthusiastic, so when we're faced with too much work, they tell me that my manner really helps to keep them motivated and calm. My boss also tells me that I'm very innovative in terms of finding new ways of working that cut out inefficiency.*

Have an example up your sleeve to justify each of your alleged strengths. An interviewer can easily ask you, *Why do you believe those are your strengths?*

For example, the Global Gadgets manager mentioned earlier in this section may go on to reply: *As just one example, our company moved offices recently. I had to co-ordinate the entire move and make sure that our server and all of the computers were set up correctly in the new office. At the same time, I dealt with all of our staff and customers to ensure that day-to-day business was not at all disrupted.*

 Try to sound confident without sounding over-confident or arrogant. If you're worried about sounding over-confident, use phrases such as *I've been told that I am . . .* and *I believe that I am . . .* rather than just saying *I am. . . .*

What are your weaknesses?

If the interviewer asks about your strengths, they will almost certainly ask about your weaknesses too. Being unable to describe any weaknesses suggests to the interviewer that you lack self-awareness or are a bit egotistical – are you really saying that you are completely perfect at everything that you do?

 Pick a couple of minor weaknesses that are of little relevance to the job. For example, if the job involves a lot of contact with customers and colleagues, then you can say that you get bored when you have to spend a lot of time working on your own. Or if the job offers you a lot of independence and flexibility, you may argue that one of your weaknesses is that you get very frustrated when you are micro-managed.

 When discussing your weaknesses, always talk about how you compensate for them, too. Describe the actions or steps that you take to ensure that your weaknesses don't affect your performance at work.

Consider this example of a weakness and how a candidate compensates for it:

My natural tendency is to make up my mind very quickly – and in the past this has got me into trouble. But I have come to realise that speed is not always appropriate so I always remind myself that I may need to collect more information and weigh up the pros and cons. Nowadays, if I am at all uncertain about a decision, I will seek input from colleagues.

What motivates you?

Employers are looking for people who are keen to make a difference to their organisation. So if you aren't terribly motivated by work and the only thing that keeps you going is the thought of leaving your workplace at the end of the day, keep that to yourself.

One trick is to say that you are motivated when you get to use the kinds of skills that the employer is looking for. For instance, if the employer requires someone with customer service skills, then – hey presto – it may be wise to say something along the lines of: *I really enjoy spending time with people and get a buzz out of dealing with customers and sorting out their problems. I hate it when I feel that I'm not doing my best on behalf of customers.* Yes, it sounds a bit cheesy, but if you say it with sincerity, it can nail you the job (if you're struggling with sincerity in interviews, Romilla Ready and Kate Burton's *Neuro-linguistic Programming For Dummies* (Wiley) helps you through by thinking positive).

Other good answers include:

- ✔ **Recognition:** While many interviewers consider it gauche to say that you are motivated by money, you can say that you like to have your good work recognised by your boss, peers, or clients.

- ✔ **Making a difference:** Especially in the charity or non-profit sector, saying that you are motivated by the pursuit of the organisation's goals is a good idea.

- ✔ **Challenge:** Another good answer is to say that you enjoy getting fully caught up in solving problems and getting to the bottom of difficult situations.

- ✔ **Self-development:** Employers like candidates who want to further their own learning and development. Do bear in mind the nature of the role that you are applying for, though. A management training scheme is likely to provide you with much more by way of development opportunities than, say, an office data entry job.

- ✔ **Money:** Only when going for a sales job should you talk about the fact that you are motivated by financial reward. In fact, many sales people are suspicious of candidates who say that they are not motivated by money and the luxuries that money can allow you to buy.

Don't just memorise one of these answers by heart. Take a moment to figure out what really motivates you – you'll sound much more genuine.

What are you passionate about?

This question is just a variant on *What motivates you?* However, the key to answering a question about passion is ensuring that your body language demonstrates not just enthusiasm but real passion. I remember observing interviews for a job as an assistant fashion buyer at a large high-street fashion retailer. All the candidates had fashion degrees and were equally knowledgeable. But the candidate who got the offer was the one whose eyes and face lit up when she talked about her passion for clothing and design and fabrics and trends and all things to do with fashion.

If being honest, a lot of people would struggle to find something to be really 'passionate' about at work. So you may be tempted to talk about a passion outside of work – perhaps a sporting interest or a community project. But if you do mention an outside interest, it allows the interviewers to wonder whether you'll be able to bring all your energies to work. So try to keep your answers within the world of work.

What are your biggest achievements?

An interviewer may ask for just one achievement or a handful – so give this question some thought beforehand. Wherever possible, keep most of your achievements work-related and focus on the benefits that you achieved for other people, such as:

- ✔ Increased customer or client satisfaction
- ✔ Greater revenues or profit
- ✔ A bigger slice of market share
- ✔ The elimination of inefficiencies or errors
- ✔ Cost reduction
- ✔ Improved relationship morale within the team or with other stakeholders
- ✔ Enhanced reputation of your employer

For example, an IT manager may say:

We were asked by our head office in the US to upgrade all of our staff's computers to a new software package. We have over 600 computers across three locations in the UK and it was imperative that we handled the migration within the space of a few days to ensure that there would be no compatibility issues. This was back in March, which is traditionally a really busy time of year for our company. I had to attend a lot of meetings with senior managers to persuade them that it was important. And I had to co-ordinate the efforts of my team to ensure that all of the computers were upgraded within those few days. It took a lot of planning and hard work, but I was really proud of the fact that we managed the migration and had only a few minor problems – and no complaints from the staff.

Don't just talk about what the achievement was – you also need to say why it was an achievement. Clearly demonstrate to the interviewer exactly what you did to make your action an achievement.

If an interviewer asks you specifically to talk about an achievement outside of work, always relate it back to the kinds of skills or characteristics that would make you a good addition to the team. And don't just assume that the link is obvious – explain the link to the interviewer. For example, passing a piano exam is evidence of your ability to focus on achieving goals that you set for yourself. Perhaps a sporting triumph is evidence of your commitment and dedication to improving your health. Or raising money for a charity is evidence of your ability to work with a team to a deadline.

What are you most proud of?

This is simply a variation of the question *What are your achievements?* The trap here is for unwary candidates who may gush about their family or accomplishments outside of work. While you may be terribly proud of your children or your relationship or having lost weight or given up smoking, try to use a work-related achievement.

Don't exaggerate your achievements. If you were involved in only a small way in a much bigger team, then a skilled interviewer may be able to see through you. Rack your brain and always pick examples where you honestly did make a significant contribution.

What is your greatest failure?

Ooh, this is a nasty question. The interviewer is setting you a big trap to fall into. The way to fend off this question is by saying that you don't think that you have ever had a 'greatest failure'.

However, saying that you've never failed is not a good enough answer on its own. So go on to talk about some minor failure that you have experienced – perhaps a particular project that did not go well or a piece of work that was not up to your usual high standards.

Try to find an example of a situation that went badly due to unforeseen circumstances. Never blame anyone else for the failure – as an interviewer can label you as someone who shirks responsibility and seeks to point the finger at other people. And try to finish off your anecdote by talking about the lesson you took from it.

Honesty is a good trait, but too much honesty can be your downfall when answering this question! If you believe that you have been guilty of a major failure – even if it was only through bad luck or circumstance – try to play it down.

Do you have any regrets?

Regret is a very strong, emotionally laden word. Again, the trap here is for unwary candidates to end up confessing major misgivings about their lives.

Unskilled interviewers often ask closed questions. But even though answering with a simple *yes* or *no* is technically correct, avoid doing so as you'll lose out on an opportunity to sell yourself.

One way to avoid the trap would be to say something like: *Sure, I have made mistakes, but I don't think that I have any real regrets. I believe that I've learnt from every situation that I've been in. And those situations and my choices in those situations have made me the person that I am.*

Alternatively, you can admit to wondering what may have happened if you had made a different decision at some time in your career. But always assert at the end of your tale that your decision was the right one to have made at the time. For example:

We had an offer from a big American conglomerate to buy our business a few years ago. But the negotiations fell through because the conglomerate was not willing to pay us fairly for our business. As it turned out, the bottom fell out of the market and the value of our shares fell. But there was no way that we could have foreseen that terrorist attacks would cause a slump in the economy. So at the time it had been the right decision.

Why should we hire you?

This question is often used to bring an interview to a close, so treat it as your opportunity to sell yourself boldly to the interviewers. A good answer may match three or four of your key skills and characteristics to the job. For example:

Your advert said that you were looking for someone who is highly numerate, has good teamworking and presentation skills, and a willingness to work hard. I hope that my experience as a financial analyst at Transworld Bank shows that I'm good with numbers. Both of the jobs I've held so far have required me to work often long hours in a close-knit team and it's something that I very much enjoy. And my boss singled out my presentation skills in my last appraisal. So I think that I am a very strong candidate.

If you want to add the icing to the cake, you can go on to mention how much you want the job. Try a bit of subtle flattery in talking about the reputation or standing of the company. Or mention some other positive reasons you want to work for the company, such as the quality of their training scheme or the fact that the business is successful and growing.

Your body language and tone of voice are doubly important when answering this key question. Make sure that you exude confidence and enthusiasm as you list the key skills and characteristics that make you the right person for the job. If confidence isn't currently one of your strongest traits, take a look at Kate Burton and Brinley Platt's *Building Confidence For Dummies* (Wiley) for good advice.

Talking about Basic Job Skills

No matter what job you are going for – a head teacher, a shop assistant, or a magazine editor – employers are looking for some fundamental skills. Being able to demonstrate that you are reliable, organised, and able to work under pressure – amongst other skills – are such prerequisites for any job that you must be ready to answer these questions.

Would you say that you're reliable?

As Homer Simpson would say: 'D'oh!' Only an idiot would say that they are not reliable. But rather than simply saying, *Yes, I am reliable*, the key here is to give an example or to explain why you think so.

 Try to figure out what the interviewer really means by 'reliable'. If the job requires staff to clock in and clock out, then perhaps the interviewer means punctual and willing to work overtime. If the job requires a high level of responsibility, then maybe the interviewer means dependable.

Consider these example answers:

- ✔ *Yes, I am a very reliable person. I've never been late for work in the 18 months that I have worked at the Grantham factory and I'm happy to do overtime if we are falling behind on our deadlines.*

- ✔ *Yes, I would say that I am very reliable. My boss knows that I'm the sort of person that he can leave to get on with an important task and I won't forget about it or quit until I have completed it.*

What's your absenteeism/sickness record like?

Employers really worry that their staff may turn up late to work or take loads of days off sick. Hopefully, you can alleviate their concerns by saying: *I have a really good absenteeism record – I have only had X days off in the last few years.* The key is for 'X' to be less than a handful.

If you have taken quite a few days off from work, make sure that you can give a compelling reason why. But go on to stress that the reason has now gone away. For example:

I did have to take four weeks off from work because I tore a ligament when I slipped on an oil patch on the shop floor. But I've now fully recovered and have a clean bill of health so it will not pose any further problems in the future.

Never lie about your sickness record, as employers frequently check up on it. Job offers are often made *subject to reference* (checking out your employment history with former employers) and a lie at this stage can lead to the employer withdrawing their offer.

How would you describe your time management skills?

For most jobs, employers are looking for *time management skills* – the ability to distinguish between what needs to be done immediately and what can wait. Of course you need to say that you have good time management skills.

A good tactic is to say that you always prioritise the most important and urgent tasks to the top of the pile. When that doesn't work, say that you enlist colleagues to help or check whether the deadline can be moved. As a final option, you can say that you simply get on with the work and stay late to get everything done.

Go on to demonstrate your time management skills by giving an example of a time when you had to prioritise between different tasks.

As an example, just the other week I had a customer who wanted an emergency order dealt with immediately at the same time as my boss needed some financial data. There was no way I could have done both, so I asked a colleague to deal with the customer order while I put together the data that my boss needed.

 Time management is ultimately the ability to distinguish between urgency and importance. *Urgency* describes whether a task needs to be done very soon or whether it can wait for a few hours or a few weeks. *Importance* describes the extent to which the task must be completed – some tasks are absolutely critical while others may be less crucial.

Are you an organised person?

Of course you are highly organised! Illustrate your organisational skills by talking about some of the methods or systems that you use to organise your work, such as:

- ✔ Making lists of tasks
- ✔ Keeping files and records on different projects
- ✔ Developing a routine or process
- ✔ Using tables, spreadsheets, computer programs, or even Gantt charts (but only talk about these if you genuinely have used them) to track progress on different pieces of work

Don't forget to prove that you really are organised by providing a short example about a project that you have organised or co-ordinated.

 Be careful not to imply that you are so organised that you would find it difficult to function without your methods and ways of working. Sometimes the world of work throws up unexpected problems and situations that you just need to tackle spontaneously.

As a subsidiary question, an interviewer may ask you: *How tidy is your desk at work?* Such a question means that the interviewer probably believes that a tidy desk is a sign of a tidy mind – so full marks go to candidates who can describe an orderly workspace.

Do you work well under pressure?

While the answer to this question is obviously yes, be careful not to exaggerate the extent to which you can cope with pressure. Try to relate your answer to the demands that the job is likely to make on you.

For example, if the job is likely to involve significant pressure, the following response may be fairly appropriate:

I positively thrive on pressure. My worst nightmare is a job that is entirely predictable and mundane. I really enjoy the fact that my job is different every day and you never know what new situations or challenges you may be facing.

If the job is more gently paced, saying that you love working under pressure may raise doubts in an interviewer's mind as to whether you would be bored by the job. So try an answer along the lines of:

I can cope with occasional bursts of having to work under pressure – for example, for the final couple of days every month it always gets a bit frantic. But for the most part, I enjoy the fact that this is a job that I can really learn and understand in detail and get good at.

If you need to demonstrate beyond a shadow of a doubt that you excel under pressure, use the acronym CAR (see the sidebar 'Driving toward great examples' at the start of this chapter) to provide an example. Make sure that the result at the end of your story is a positive one!

Would you say that you're creative?

An interviewer may ask if you are creative or innovative – and for all practical purposes, you can treat these as the same question. Your answer to this question depends on the nature of the job you are being interviewed for. If you're applying for a job requiring high levels of artistic ability and visual creativity (such as a graphic designer or an advertising executive), then say yes and have ready a portfolio with at least a couple of examples of how you have demonstrated your creativity.

Bear in mind that employers are looking for not just creative ideas, but actual tangible products, designs, and inventions. So make sure that your examples describe how you turned an idea in your head into a solution that benefited your team or organisation.

If you're not applying for a job that demands high levels of creativity and you feel that creativity really is not one of your strong points, then this is one occasion when you should feel comfortable being honest in saying so. But go on to stress some of your other key strengths and qualities.

If the job is a managerial one, you can get away with saying that creativity is not one of your key strengths. I have heard a number of managers impress interviewers by saying that while creativity is not one of their key strengths, they try to create an atmosphere in their teams that encourages creativity through brainstorming, running workshops and away days, and supporting the ideas that members of the team have.

Would you say you're good with detail?

For the majority of candidates, the answer to this question should be a yes. Of course employers don't want to take slip-shod people on board.

If the job requires highly detailed work, give a simple example of how you ensure that your work is of a consistently high quality:

In my job it's really important to get all of the numbers right, so I always double check the data after I have entered it. And I'm glad to say that in my two years in the job so far, no one has ever found an error in my calculations.

The exception to this general rule is managers. For managers in middling to senior roles, employers often expect them to pay attention to the big picture rather than getting too bogged down in detail. So if you already manage a medium to large team of people – say at least a couple of dozen or more people – then you can get away with saying:

I have to admit that detail isn't one of my strong points. I try to keep focused on the big picture. However, I always make sure that I have good people in my team who can handle the detail.

How do you respond to change?

Interviewers do not want to end up hiring an inflexible and unadaptable employee. I'm sure you know the type – the grumpy person who complains about how things are 'nowadays' and constantly reminisces about the 'good old days' before such and such a change.

The world of work is changing quickly – with factors at play such as globalisation, mergers and acquisitions, change programmes, and efficiency drives. Talking about how you have coped with one of these changes will illustrate your ability to deal with change.

Make sure that you can show that you're willing to adapt to new circumstances, maybe along the lines of:

A couple of people left our team in the space of just a week, which meant that we were heavily understaffed for a period of over a month. The rest of the team had to readjust our shifts to ensure that the helpdesk remained manned at all times. I volunteered for a few additional shifts because I knew that our customers would otherwise have no one to sort out their problems.

Another tactic showing that you not only cope with change, but excel at it, is talking about how you have helped others through change. Perhaps you had colleagues who were uncertain of a new rota, but you talked them round. Or you volunteered to work on a project team, committee, or task force responsible for some part of the change process. Either of these examples demonstrates that you are not only reactively able to cope with change, but can proactively contribute to it.

How are you with new technology?

A variation on questioning your ability to cope with change, this question about technology tends to get asked more of older candidates. If you think about it, new technology is being introduced all the time – from new computers and laptops to mobile phones and electronic key cards. Worrisome employers don't want to hire people who struggle to master even the very basics of how to use them.

Give as concrete an example as possible of getting to grips with some new facet of technology that has been introduced into your workplace:

We used to use transparent acetates and old-fashioned overhead projectors for teaching seminars. But the university decided to introduce laptops and projectors and asked us all to prepare our materials using PowerPoint. I'm pleased to say that after attending the briefing sessions on how to use the new technology, I've become a real fan of this new way of working.

What software packages are you familiar with?

If you are going for a role where software packages are important, then it's usually a good idea to list them somewhere on your CV. If an employer then asks you about your level of proficiency with different packages, make sure that you can give examples of what feats you can perform on each. For example:

I'm responsible for creating the monthly department newsletter, which usually means using that package to format and tabulate other people's contributions. I also have to import images and create detailed proposal documents for my manager. And I can merge lists of contacts with letter templates to create marketing mailshots.

Even the most seasoned of executives is usually assumed to have a passing knowledge of how to use a computer. Partners in top City law firms and senior managers with budgets of hundreds of millions of pounds are expected to read and send their own e-mails and type a few words into a document. So if you can't do at least these two basic tasks, make sure you find someone to teach you how!

If you really don't know anything about computers, then try to go on a training course or get a colleague or friend to teach you how to use the basics of the Microsoft Office package. Microsoft is by far the most popular software developer in the workplace, so is a good one to start with.

How would you rate yourself as . . .?

An interviewer can ask you to rate yourself on a number of criteria – such as your skills as a leader, a team player, a teacher, or a researcher. Obviously, you need to begin by saying that you are a good leader, team player, or whatever. Don't let modesty get in the way of selling yourself – you can bet that other candidates are making all sorts of wild claims about how great they are.

To back up your claim, do go on to tell a short anecdote or cite an example as to why you think you rate yourself so highly. If you have won any awards or ever received any commendations or positive feedback from colleagues or customers, then this may be the time to mention it.

If an interviewer asks for a numerical rating, avoid giving yourself a score of 10/10. Trying to claim that you are perfect will come across as incredibly bigheaded. A score of 8/10 is more reasonable. Go on to say something like: *I believe that I'm very good at X, but there is always more to learn.* This response shows an ounce of humility and willingness to improve even further – good traits to have in an employee.

Chapter 5

Talking about Problems, Perceptions, and People

*E*mployers want to hire self-motivated workers with good people skills. If you were hiring someone, wouldn't you want those qualities, too?

In this chapter, I talk about how to answer questions focusing on motivation and dealing with others, and how to successfully bat off the sort of questions that niggle away at the back of an interviewer's mind.

Overcoming Interviewers' Common Worries

Because employers are a worrisome lot, you have the task of convincing them you have no characteristics that should cause them undue concern. Sure, their job advert focuses on the positive qualities they're looking for in their candidate of choice, but be aware that employers are apt to think about the negative characteristics, as well. After all, I'm sure you know plenty of people who have bad tempers, who are difficult to manage and shy away from hard work, are boring to be around, and so on. In this section, I focus on how you can convince interviewers you have none of these negative characteristics.

What makes you lose your temper?

If you can truthfully say that you never lose your temper at work, then by all means say so. Explain to the interviewer exactly how or why you manage to keep your temper at bay when you're at work. For example:

I'm not the kind of person who ever gets angry at work. Anger just isn't productive and even in a crisis it's more important to figure out what can be done to sort out the situation than to shout and scream and point the finger of blame at people.

If you do occasionally lose your temper, word your response as carefully as possible:

I guess that sometimes I do let my frustration show. For example, when colleagues promise to do something and then let me down at the last moment, I have been known to have a few terse words with them.

How do you respond to authority?

No one wants to take on an argumentative employee who's resistant to authority. But your answer to this question – or its variant *How well do you take direction?* – may depend on the nature of the organisation.

In traditional and hierarchical organisations where employees are expected to know their place and defer to people more senior, show your keen appreciation of the need to defer to authority in your answer:

I respect authority and enjoy having a straightforward reporting relationship where my boss gives me guidelines on what I can or cannot do. In my current job, I know exactly what decisions I can make. For bigger decisions or larger items of spend, I always check with my supervisor. If I were to be taken on in this role, I would like to sit down with my manager as soon as possible to establish how best to work together.

If you think that your interview is with a progressive organisation, position yourself as a more freethinking candidate:

I have the utmost respect for authority, but I'm not the kind of person who will mindlessly do everything that my manager tells me. If I don't understand something or think that a decision isn't in the best interests of the team, I'll ask questions until I'm satisfied with my manager's response. But ultimately if I feel that management has listened to my questions or objections, then I have to respect their decision and get on with it.

How do you deal with disappointment?

Being able to deal with setbacks and disappointment is a really important quality. Life (and work) doesn't always go the way you want it to, and candidates who admit to giving up immediately are frankly a pain to work with! Employers want people who live by the adage 'If at first you don't succeed, try, try again.'

Of course I don't enjoy being disappointed, but rather than dwell on the past I try to focus on the future. As such, I always try to make the best of any situation. If I feel that I can do anything to better the situation, then I try to do it. But if it looks as if the chance has gone, then I try to see what I can learn from it.

If you can, give an example of a situation when an initial rejection or rebuttal actually spurred you on to make a greater effort or take further steps that eventually led to success.

When I first wanted to work in music production, I sent off my CV to more than 80 companies and didn't get an interview from a single one. But I knew that I really wanted to work in the industry so I took my CV round to some of their offices and literally knocked on companies' doors. I physically visited 30 or 40 companies and got offered a week's unpaid work experience at one of them, and at the end of the week they offered me a job.

How do you cope with job stress?

The interviewer isn't asking you *whether* you can cope with stressful situations at work, but *how* you cope with them. Engaging in sports or exercise is probably the most socially acceptable way of letting off steam: *No matter how bad the day*

I've had – perhaps it's due to a difficult case or just too much to do – when I get home, I get changed and go for a 20-minute jog. Whenever I do that, I can literally feel the tension leaving my body.

Other ways of unwinding may include:

- ✔ Socialising with friends or colleagues.
- ✔ Cooking dinner for friends.
- ✔ Talking about a day's stressful activities with a friend or partner at home.
- ✔ Engaging in relaxing activities such meditation, yoga, or having a bath with scented oils.

Think about how your chosen method of unwinding may be viewed by the interviewers. An activity that seems completely acceptable in one organisational culture may be frowned upon in another. For example, interviewers at an investment bank or a fashion house are more likely to view having a drink in a favourable light, while they may be less impressed with people who go home to meditate. If you want to get maximum brownie points, emphasise any common interests you have with the interviewers or the people who typically work in their organisation.

What's your attitude to taking risks?

The key to answering this question is to think about the employer's likely attitude to risks. After all, would you want to put your life in the hands of a surgeon or airline pilot who admits to living on the edge? As such, industries such as manufacturing, oil and gas, airlines, and the health professions are probably very conservative about risk-taking because of the very real possibility of physical injury or death. Here's an example of an answer that fits well in the oil industry:

I'm a strong believer in never having to take risks. Ours is a difficult job and it's imperative that everyone has had a full health and safety briefing. I always assign two people to check that the equipment is sound before we proceed with the drilling.

Other companies may actively encourage their employees to take calculated risks if they feel that the downside is very much outweighed by the possible upside – and at the end of the day, they may only be risking a small chunk of their budget rather than loss of life or limb!

When talking about your attitude to risk, bear in mind that a world of difference exists between a calculated risk and a complete shot in the dark:

I don't mind taking risks if I feel that I have done whatever I can to establish the pros and cons. At the end of the day, most business decisions are slightly uncertain, but if the financial projections don't look too bad and my gut feeling is good, then I'll take a chance. Generally, my instincts have been sound and the majority of our projects make money.

Ours is a work hard, play hard culture – how do you feel about that?

Employers like to hire in their own image. You've probably heard of the *Old Boys' Network* – chaps from stuffy schools and colleges hiring other chaps who went to the same schools and colleges. But even if the interviewers didn't go to a prestigious school, they still like to hire people who are like them.

If an employer describes the company culture, then obviously say that you think you'd fit into that culture really well. If you'd be happy working and playing hard – which probably means working a 12-hour day and then going out drinking with your colleagues – then tell the interviewers exactly that.

If you really don't feel that way, this probably isn't the right job for you. And admitting that you don't feel that way will almost certainly count against your candidacy.

Tell me something interesting about yourself

Hmm, this is a tricky one because the interviewer wants someone who has something to talk about outside of work.

And this is a perfectly understandable question, too – would you want to work with someone who had nothing to talk about apart from work?

Do you have a skill or talent that you can talk about? Perhaps you have an unusual hobby or interest. Or maybe you have achieved something remarkable. What you talk about almost doesn't matter, so long as you can talk about something outside of the workplace.

Consider these genuine examples that I've heard:

- ✔ A call centre supervisor said that she was taking dance classes and her ambition was to be able to do the splits.

- ✔ A management consultant revealed that he used to be an aerobics instructor when he was at university.

- ✔ A primary school teacher mentioned that he had a turntable at home and spent occasional weekends DJ-ing at local nightclubs.

Be careful about trying to be funny. Humour is really difficult to judge – especially when you don't know people very well. Innuendoes can go down like a ton of bricks while an ironic statement may get taken at face value. For example, I once met an interviewer who thought a candidate was being deadly serious when he joked that he was wearing his girlfriend's underwear! So try to think of an interesting fact about yourself rather than answering this question in a flippant fashion.

What would you say your Unique Selling Point is?

A *Unique Selling Point* (USP) is a bit of marketing jargon. The interviewer is asking what makes you unique and why you stand out from the other candidates. As you can never know exactly what skills and experiences the other candidates have, talk about how you differ from (and are a better candidate than) your *peers* (people that you know at your own level in your industry). Or you can argue that your combination of skills and characteristics makes you unique.

Consider a couple of examples:

> ✔ *I've been working as a beauty consultant for a few years now. But without wanting to sound too bigheaded, I've noticed that I tend to pick up information about new products a lot more quickly than just about any other consultant I've worked with. And that enables me to sell the products much more successfully.*

> ✔ *What hopefully makes me unique is the fact that I have bundles of enthusiasm and a real ambition to progress. I am ever so keen to get on and build a career in this industry, and I think that you would find it difficult to find someone who has my energy and willingness to work hard.*

Seeing Yourself As Others See You

A common tactic employers draw upon is to ask you how different people may rate or describe you. The knack in answering this question is to talk up the positive remarks that others may say or have said about you while playing down some of the negative comments.

Don't lie. If everyone you work with says that you are really bad at a particular skill, avoid mentioning that skill. Remember that employers frequently check references as a condition of offering you a job. A reference that describes you as the complete opposite of how you have described yourself can be a real deal breaker.

What would your boss say about you?

A good answer alludes to some of the skills or qualities that the interviewers are looking for. Your cause won't be helped if your boss thought you were great at analysing quantitative data on your own if the job requires someone who can work on qualitative data in a team.

Treat this question as if the interviewers had asked you the question: *What would your boss say are your good points?* – there's no point in emphasising your weaknesses unless the interviewers specifically ask for them.

She would say that I'm someone who is totally reliable and a safe pair of hands for any difficult work that she might need doing. She also asks me to deputise for her in committee meetings.

If you are too extravagant in your claims as to how good your boss thought you were, the interviewers are more likely to ask you to justify your assertions with an example or two.

In your last appraisal, what was said about your performance?

Unfortunately, appraisals often have the tendency of focusing more on development areas and weaknesses than what you are good at, but your answer to this question should focus on your achievements rather than your failings.

I was pleased that my manager said that I had made significant progress toward becoming an area manager. I had succeeded in restoring good relationships with our suppliers and putting in place new service level agreements with them. Our performance is also rated across five key skill categories and I was pleased that I was rated as 'above average' on four of them, and ' exceptional' on one.

Another common variant on this question is: *What goals did your boss set for you in your last appraisal?* If this question is asked, describe the goals briefly, but then spend most of the time talking about the actions or steps that you have been taking (or intend to take) to reach those goals.

My boss thought that I should aim to boost my department's staff satisfaction score from its current 75% to 80%. I now plan to have a number of away days for the entire team to discuss our quarterly targets and how best to achieve them. And I am putting in place a coaching programme to ensure that the junior managers are spending at least an hour a week talking to each of their direct reports about the issues affecting them.

How do you think you can improve on your performance?

This question often follows, *In your last appraisal, what was said about your performance?* (see the preceding section for advice on how to answer that question). The interviewer is now asking you specifically about any areas for development or improvement.

Talk about not only why you failed to reach some of your targets but also what you have since planned to do to reach them in the future. And, if possible, talk about what benefits you are seeing as a result of your new approach.

My manager felt that while I'm very good at getting my work done, I need to be a bit more strategic in my outlook. He said that I have a tendency to focus on my own immediate piece of work, but not to look at the bigger picture. Since then I have been making a concerted effort to talk to the rest of the team more frequently to ensure that my own work ties more closely into the overall project's objectives. It has already helped us to spot some potential problems and deal with them before they affect the quality of our output.

What would your colleagues say about you?

This question is a common alternative to *What would your boss say about you?* (a question covered earlier in this chapter). While your boss may say that you are better than others in the team at certain skills, your team mates are unlikely to use the same sort of language.

Think about the contribution that you make to the team. What is it that you can always be relied upon to do? Or what sorts of problems or issues do your colleagues tend to come to you with? Make sure that your answer marks you out as an invaluable part of the team:

> ✔ *I think they would say that I tend to play the devil's advocate. I'm the kind of person who can see the problems with an idea or argument quite quickly. That doesn't mean that*

*I'll automatically be negative about an idea, but it does
mean that I can ask the right questions and point out the
flaw so that we can think about how to make the idea more
workable instead.*

✔ *My colleagues tend to see me as the person that they can
come and talk to when they're feeling down. If they're
having a bad day, they know that I lend a sympathetic ear.
Sometimes they just take the opportunity to vent their frustrations and let off steam. But sometimes they are stumped
by a problem and I tend to be quite good at seeing how
they might deal with a situation.*

How would your team describe you?

This question only applies if you manage or are sometimes
responsible for a team of more junior people. You're being
asked to rate your own ability as a leader, manager, or
supervisor.

*I think my team would say that I'm a fair and open manager.
I try to get to know what sort of work they enjoy and what they
are good or bad at. I try to give them work that they will find
challenging but at the same time enjoyable. Once I've set my
team a piece of work, I try to avoid checking up on them too
much. At the same time, I have an 'open door' policy so that
they can come to me with any problems whenever they need to.*

Other key words used to describe desirable management
styles include 'empowering' and 'democratic'.

How do you think your friends would describe you?

Your friends are unlikely to comment on your work skills. So
focus more on the qualities and characteristics that make you
a good person to know. Good qualities to mention include:

✔ A friendly and outgoing nature

✔ Sense of humour

   ✔ Reliability or loyalty

   ✔ Tact and ability to keep confidences

   ✔ Persistence, ambition, or determination

   ✔ Willingness to get up after being knocked down

My friends would say that I'm quite ambitious. I'm the kind of person who sets goals and then sets out to achieve them – for example, I didn't want to get too much into debt while at university so kept looking until I found a part-time job that I could juggle at the same time as my studies. But while I'm ambitious, I don't take myself too seriously. I'm good fun to be around and have a strongly ironic sense of humour.

Pick traits or attributes relevant for the job. For example, if applying for a job as a receptionist at a doctor's surgery, saying that your friends would say that you have a great sense of humour and are a constant practical joker may be less helpful than the fact they find you tactful and a pillar of strength when they are feeling unhappy.

Everyone has some kind of fault – what would other people say your faults are?

In this question, 'other people' can refer to your colleagues, your friends, or your team. If you have answered any of the previous handful of questions by describing the good stuff about yourself (as you should always do), a particularly canny interviewer then tends to follow up by asking about some of the bad stuff, too. However, the word 'fault' is quite strong – it suggests that you have a major flaw in your character. So beat the interviewers at their own game by preparing a story about a minor failing instead.

When talking about any faults, weaknesses, or areas for improvement, it's critical that you talk about the steps or actions that you take to limit or compensate for them, as shown in the following examples:

   ✔ *Of course I'm not perfect. I know that I can get very enthusiastic about new ideas and can come across to some people as a bit impatient. It's just that I get too keen about a project that I think has real benefits. So nowadays I try to keep in mind that I need to slow down to avoid bulldozing others.*

✔ *When I'm under pressure, I know that I can get a little uncommunicative. If I've got too much to do, I like to get my head down and get on with it. So on those rare occasions, people have said that I'm not my usually fun self. But when I've got the work out of the way, I quickly snap out of it.*

Discussing Your People Skills

If employers had to pick the most important category of skills in choosing between candidates, they'd probably pick interpersonal skills. Unless you are working in a sealed room without even a telephone in it (which is a highly unlikely situation – how many jobs can you name that don't involve any interaction whatsoever with other human beings?), you'll need good interpersonal skills to deal with colleagues, clients and customers, and suppliers.

In particular roles, such as sales, you may need highly developed pitching and negotiation skills. But the questions in this section are relevant to just about everyone.

Do you prefer to work on your own or in a team?

Team working skills are highly prized in most organisations. At the same time though, don't imply that you are completely hopeless and unable to concentrate when a task requires you to work independently of others.

This question has no single right answer. Your approach to the question depends on the nature of the job. Take a few seconds to think about how much time the job would require you to spend working in a team versus working on your own.

Belbin's team types

Dr Meredith Belbin established that most people tend to fall into one of nine types when contributing to a team. Very briefly, these types are:

- ✓ **Plant**: A person who comes up with ideas. Others tend to view them as creative and imaginative.

- ✓ **Co-ordinator**: A chairperson who is good at getting others involved and organised.

- ✓ **Monitor Evaluator**: A sharp mind, this person is good at seeing the flaws and faults in others' arguments.

- ✓ **Completer Finisher**: A conscientious person who is good at attending to detail and meeting deadlines.

- ✓ **Implementer**: A person who is good at turning vague ideas into practical actions.

- ✓ **Resource Investigator**: A sociable person with a good network of contacts who uses that network to discuss and explore ideas.

- ✓ **Shaper**: A driven person who has the determination to overcome obstacles.

- ✓ **Team worker**: A co-operative person who is good at listening and enjoys getting on with the work that they are given.

- ✓ **Specialist**: Often a single-minded person who provides expertise or knowledge that others do not have.

These team type descriptors are quite widespread in business. But if you want to refer to your team type, first ensure that the interviewer is familiar with the typology by asking, *Are you familiar with Belbin's team types?* before launching into a description of where you believe you fit in.

Make sure that you are very familiar with your team type before trying to talk about it. Nothing is worse than a candidate who tries to talk about Belbin only for the interviewer to find out that they don't really know anything about the strengths and weaknesses associated with that type.

In reality, very few people can be labelled as one of the nine types all the time – people tend to shift between two or three types depending on the situation and their mood. But the typology serves as a useful framework for discussing differences in behaviour. If you want to read more on the topic, then simply type 'Belbin team types' into an Internet search engine.

If, for example, the job requires you to work almost constantly in a team, an answer such as the following may be appropriate:

I can work on my own, but to be honest I get the biggest buzz from working in a fast-paced team. I like having people around me constantly to bounce ideas off. When there are lots of creative people around you, it doesn't feel like work to me.

If a job requires extensive periods of working independently but also intense bursts of working in a team, try:

To be honest I get my best work done when I can sit quietly and think on my own – so that's why I'm attracted to this job because you're offering the successful candidate the opportunity to work from home for up to three days a week. However, I couldn't work from home all week because I'd miss the human contact – so again this job is attractive because I would get the opportunity to share ideas with the rest of the team on those days in the office.

We all have a team role – what would you say your role tends to be?

Are you a leader or a follower? Are you the person who comes up with the ideas or the person who can more easily see the flaws in other people's ideas? Do you tend to look at the long-term possibilities of an idea or are you more attuned to any immediate practical applications? Whatever the case, make sure that you can say that you have something of value to add to a team.

As with most interview questions, no single right answer exists. Relate your answer to the nature of the job. For example, if you are applying for a supervisory or managerial job, talk about the fact that others tend to defer to you and that you enjoy being in charge. Or if interviewed for a technical role, talk about occasions when you have introduced your specialist knowledge into team discussions.

These team-related examples give you some ideas:

> ✔ *I tend to be an optimist and motivator within the team. While I admit that I may not be the most creative person in the team, I can spot a good idea when I hear it and I do my best to get everybody talking about it. And after a team meeting, I can be relied upon to follow up on the idea, do a bit of research on it, and canvass opinion across the rest of the organisation before the next team meeting.*

> ✔ *I'm incredibly flexible when it comes to working in teams and one of the things that I most enjoy about my current job is the fact that I don't have a fixed role. I think I'd get bored if I was always doing the same thing in the team. But the fact that we are constantly shifting roles on different projects means that I get a lot of variety. And this is one of the features that attracts me to this role with you.*

If you want to get more technical about your role in a team, refer to your *team type descriptor*. See the sidebar 'Belbin's team types' for more information.

Do you have good presentation skills?

Be careful of falling into the trap of saying that you are fantastic at absolutely everything. If good presentation skills are one of the key handful of skills necessary for the job, then of course you need to talk up your ability. But if you would only need to give presentations occasionally, be more measured in your response.

Some people are good at standing up and talking to a large audience on the spur of the moment with no preparation; others need to prepare their PowerPoint demonstration, write their speech, and rehearse it. Which approach do you need to be good at in the job that you're applying for?

Compare the following two examples relating to different jobs:

> ✔ *Standing up and giving presentations is something that I really enjoy and I've had a lot of practice at it, so yes, I think I have excellent presentation skills. I do lots of different presentations from standing up in team meetings and*

> *giving a brief summary on my week's work to writing out a speech for an hour-long keynote presentation at a legal conference last month, which they actually filmed and put onto a DVD for the delegates.*
>
> ✔ *I would say that I have quite solid presentation skills. We pick a teacher every week to give a seminar to the whole college. When it's my turn, I always spend a couple of evenings creating a PowerPoint presentation and writing bullet points onto pieces of card. Doing that preparation means that I can get my point across in a clear and effective way.*

The first example is more appropriate for someone who needs to do a lot of public speaking while the second example is better for someone who only needs to stand up in public occasionally.

How would you rate your customer service skills?

The key to success in dealing with customers is having good listening skills and being able to grit your teeth and stay calm no matter how angry or unpleasant customers are. Make sure that you mention these qualities when constructing your answer. And don't forget to give a solid example of putting your customer service skills into action.

I think I have very good customer skills because I always put myself in their shoes and think how I would like to be treated if I were a customer. Just last week, I had a customer who came into the store wanting to buy one of the new season's skirts in her size. But we didn't have a size 14 on the sales floor and I couldn't find one in the storeroom. I suggested that she try one of the other stores in the city. I called a couple of the other branches and found one that had a size 14 in stock and told them to put it to one side for her. But she was a tourist and didn't know how to get from our store to the other location so I went out with her to the street to hail her a cab to take her there.

One of the best examples to give is dealing with an initially angry or unhappy customer's complaint and ending up with a happy or even delighted customer. Or think about a time when you went out of your way to satisfy a customer's requests even though it was not necessarily your job to do so. Don't give an example that involves having to refer a customer to your manager or another department as it demonstrates to the interviewer that you are the type of person who shirks their problems. Similarly, don't let your story end up with the customer storming off because you couldn't resolve the situation for them.

If meeting customers on a daily basis, you need to show that you are using these skills all the time. Make sure that you pick a recent example from the last couple of weeks or months. Going any further back in time may suggest to the interviewers that you only choose to use your customer service skills on special occasions!

How are you at handling conflict?

This is a trick question, because simply wading in and saying that you are very good at handling conflict may imply that you get into lots of arguments and disagreements with other people. Unless you are applying to be an armed peacekeeper, a more sensible tactic may be to start off by saying that you don't tend to get into many conflict situations.

Most people tend to be fairly bad at dealing with conflict. Some people are too aggressive and get others' backs up while others are too passive and back down when they should be standing up for their rights. A good balance between the two is to be able to explain that you try to assert yourself on key points but remain flexible on others.

When I'm dealing with customers, I realise that it's my job to take some of the flak when they are unhappy. If you try to argue back with them, that will only escalate the situation, so I always apologise on behalf of the company and try to find out what went wrong. I find that if you are sincere enough in your apology and explain that you are going to do your best to try to sort the situation out, the customer quickly calms down.

We need someone who is tactful and diplomatic – how does that profile fit you?

Are you the kind of person who can tell a white lie or bite their lip in order to spare someone's feelings? Or are you the kind of person who would just blurt out, *Yes, that dress does make you look fat.* While most organisations would be disappointed with people who tell lies or don't speak their mind all the time, they do want employees to be able to choose the right time and place to speak up.

I'm very diplomatic because I understand that speaking your mind may not always be the best course of action. Sometimes you need to think about the right time and place to make certain comments. For instance, when you want to criticise someone, I think you should always do it one-to-one and in private rather than openly, in front of other people.

 An interviewer may ask if you have ever lied at work. Be careful when answering, as different organisations have different views on the extent to which it is appropriate or acceptable to hide the truth. For example, most businesses would say that lying to customers outside of the company is more acceptable than lying to colleagues within the company. Only a fine line separates a white lie from an outright falsification, so think through your answer carefully.

How do you take personal criticism?

A person who can't take personal criticism is a pain to work with. No one wants to work with someone who automatically takes offence at the slightest suggestion that her work is not perfect. And, no one likes a person whose bottom lip starts to wobble because he perceives criticism as an attack on his self-esteem. Here's a good response:

I welcome constructive criticism if I think that it is justified. If I think that my manager has a valid point, then I take it on board and think about how to improve my performance the next time that situation crops up. But if I don't think that it is fair, then I will keep asking questions until I understand where my manager's coming from. And if I don't agree with all of their points or feel that they have got the wrong end of the stick, then I try to explain my point of view.

Be careful not to give the interviewers the impression that you are a complete doormat. A world of a difference exists between listening to fair and constructive criticism and paying attention to all manner of criticism whether it is warranted or not.

Chapter 6

Getting to Grips with Questions about Your Work

In This Chapter
▶ Talking about your current and previous jobs
▶ Discussing your current or previous employer

*T*he most commonly asked questions in a job interview are about the past, present, and future of your career. Interviewers want to examine the relevance of your previous roles in relation to the vacancy they're seeking to fill. Interviewers also want to understand why you are looking to leave (or have already left) your current employer and join their company. And they want to see if you have thought through what you want from the rest of your career.

In this chapter, I help you talk up your career history and explain what you want from not only your next job but also the rest of your working life.

Responding to Questions about Your Work

Your CV (refer to Chapter 2 for more on this) is only a brief summary of your entire career and cannot possibly capture all the activities that you actually did in each of your previous jobs. And most interviewers would rather 'hear it from the horse's mouth' than read the details – so be sure to memorise your career history and be ready to talk through each of the jobs on your CV.

Relate all your answers to the kinds of skills and characteristics that the interviewers are looking for in the role you're being interviewed for. Don't simply rehearse the same answers for all the different interviews that you go to, as different organisations may want slightly different skills.

What does your day-to-day job involve?

Don't get bogged down in describing all the details of your current job. If you list every single action or duty that you have, you will quickly bore the interviewer. The way to shine when answering this question is to focus on three, four – or at most five – key areas of responsibility that you think the interviewers may be looking for.

> ✔ *I am responsible for all our company's graphic design needs. In practice, this breaks down into three main areas. The first is to produce the monthly newsletter that goes out to all our customers. So I have to chase different departments to write the sections of the newsletter and then assemble them in an attractive format. Secondly, I work with the marketing team when they want to design new logos to accompany new products. And thirdly, I'm responsible for ensuring that all the correspondence that goes out to customers is consistent with our brand by checking up on employees at all levels of the company and educating them about our standard document formats.*

> ✔ *As a senior associate, I run a team of six lawyers in the corporate law practice working directly with the partner. I am responsible for the day-to-day management of the lawyers, which includes managing their workload, ensuring that their work is of a high quality, and coaching and developing them so that they can take on work of an increasingly more difficult nature. I also act as a liaison between the firm and the client, making sure that the client is happy. But most importantly I'm looking out for opportunities to deepen the client relationship so that the client will use us for other transactions.*

Prepare an answer to explain the day-to-day workings of all your jobs to date, not just your last one. An interviewer can conceivably go on to ask: *What did your other jobs entail?* or

*Please tell me about the main duties that you performed in each
of your jobs.*

How did you get your last job?

You often hear people saying that job hunting is a job in itself.
Answering this question is an opportunity for you to show
your tenacity in chasing down a job. If you went through a
lengthy and difficult selection process, you may win a few
extra points for explaining the steps that you had to go
through to get the job.

*Last year our company announced that it was restructuring the
company and creating six new regional manager positions. All
the 300 or so existing area managers were invited to apply,
which involved completing a ten-page application form and sub-
mitting various letters of reference. I believe that about 200 of us
applied for the new positions. I put in my application and was
invited to attend an assessment centre in which we had to complete a battery of psychometric tests. We were also interviewed
by a psychologist and had to give a presentation to one of the
regional directors. The successful applicants were then invited to
a second-round panel interview, which consisted of the three
regional directors, a finance representative, and the director of
human resources. At the end of a rather gruelling two-hour interview, I was successful in securing the position.*

If applying for a position requiring a lot of networking on the
job – such as in sales or business development – you may
again win Brownie points by talking about how you networked
your way into the job.

*I had been reading the appointments sections of newspapers
for a while to see if any opportunities existed in my field, but
hadn't seen any for ages. So I started ringing people I knew and
explained that I was looking to move out of the finance sector
and into consumer goods. I didn't ask them for a job, but asked
if they knew any people who could talk to me about the consumer goods industry. It took quite a while and a lot of phone
calls and meetings, but eventually I found my way to the managing director of my current employer who was willing to give
someone like me a chance.*

What do you like about your current job?

Even though the perks of the job may really be your favourite bit – such as a subsidised canteen, six weeks annual holiday, and an easy-going boss – a *good* answer focuses on the fact that your current job gives you the opportunity to exercise certain skills. A *great* answer would focus on how you exercise skills that are uncannily similar to the ones mentioned in the job advert.

> ✔ *I like the fact that I'm helping line managers to make decisions that can have a very large impact on the success or failure of the company. Of course I spend some of my time analysing the weekly financial performance of individual departments. But once I have those numbers, I can get out and spend time helping the line managers to make decisions about how to allocate their budgets and spend their time. And the fact that I'm working with non-accountants to help them understand the principles of financial management is probably the most satisfying part of my job.*

> ✔ *What I enjoy most about my job is that each day can be very different. One day I can be carrying out safety checks and inspections on the machines and equipment. The next, I could be installing or upgrading electrical circuits. Or I could be working with the managers to develop improvements to the maintenance procedures.*

What do you dislike about your work?

An interviewer may find it hard to swallow if you claim that you enjoy every single aspect of your work. Everyone has minor dislikes or frustrations with their work and you need to be ready to talk about some of them. Your tactic can be to talk about factors outside of your control – for example, unwieldy organisational procedures to follow or inefficient systems that do not allow you to work as productively as you would like to. Using this tactic may be a good idea if you are fairly certain that the situation is different in the interviewers' organisation.

You don't want to sound permanently unhappy in your job, or you can come across as a grumpy individual that the interviewers would be better off rejecting. Be very careful to make it clear to the interviewers that you rarely feel frustrated or irritated by these factors.

In my current role, I have to travel to all the branches in the entire north of England, so I spend about four days out of five on the road. I used to enjoy it but now the appeal is starting to wear off and I have increasingly been thinking about taking a head office role. One of the attractions of coming here today is that I would be based in the Leeds office at least three days a week.

When asked about what you dislike in your job, you may want to talk about a necessary evil that your job entails, such as the need to complete an incessant amount of paperwork. But be careful to ensure that paperwork (or any other element of a job) isn't going to be a key part of the job before talking about how much you dislike it!

I don't think there is anything in particular that I really dislike in my job. I enjoy meeting suppliers and building the relationships between our company and each of theirs. I guess if I had to think of something, then it's the paperwork that I have to complete once I get back to the office. But I realise that the documentation is important and once I've got it done, I can focus on the tasks that I enjoy more.

How is your performance measured?

Although this question asks you to talk about the way in which your performance is measured, what the interviewer is really interested in is the extent to which you fall behind, meet, or exceed your targets or objectives.

Most people have targets or objectives set on an annual or perhaps quarterly basis. If you are not familiar with your goals, dig out your last appraisal in order to prepare the answer to this question. In some jobs, such as a call centre operator or a retail sales assistant, you may even have daily targets to meet. But interviewers are not interested in your performance on a day-to-day basis; your performance over a longer period of time such as a month or a quarter is what really matters.

My performance is measured against about a dozen criteria, but I have two main objectives that make up over 70 per cent of whether I get an end-of-year bonus or not. One objective is my management of a cost budget and the other is the extent to which I minimise manufacturing downtime. In the first quarter of the year, I'm ahead of both targets by between three to four per cent.

If you are falling behind with any of your targets or objectives, make sure that you have good reasons to explain why.

I have three main objectives for the year. The first is to generate £100,000 worth of new business. The second is to deliver £180,000 of consulting work in a year. And the third is to accrue a certain number of personal development points by reading books, attending workshops, and finding out about competitors' activities. In the first half of the year, I achieved 113 per cent of my consulting delivery target. I'm also ahead of the game in terms of my personal development points. However, I've only managed to generate 85 per cent of my new business target – but that's mainly because I've been so busy doing consultancy work that I haven't had the chance to attend many conferences and to network.

Many managers are measured against a balanced business scorecard, comprising elements such as financial performance, customer satisfaction, staff satisfaction, and innovation. If you're measured in this way, make sure you can describe your performance against target for all the major elements of your job. And if you're not meeting your target in any particular area, you can bet that the interviewer will want to talk about it in more detail – so be ready with some answers.

What have you learned in each of your previous jobs?

This question can be taken in two different ways. The interviewer may be asking, *What skills have you learned in each of your previous jobs?* or *What lessons have you learned in each of your previous jobs?* Rather than making an assumption, clarify what information the interviewer is seeking. So begin by asking: *Would you rather I talk about the skills I picked up in each of my jobs or the lessons that I learned?*

If the interviewer is interested in skills rather than lessons, talk about a transferable skill you picked up in each job relevant to the job you're applying for:

Going back to the beginning, Robinson and Partners was my first job, so I learnt a lot about working on projects, setting goals, and working to deadlines. At Recruitment Solutions, I got the opportunity to hone my client-handling skills because I was working with a wide range of companies, from small companies to large employers. In my current role, I am supervising two trainees, so I've become very good at delegating work clearly and then coaching and explaining when they have any problems.

Here's an example of a response if the interviewer is more interested in your philosophical take on your career:

In my job at Mail Express, I learnt that you can't let people down. When you say you're going to do something, then you just have to get on with it and do it. There was one occasion when I stayed in the office until after midnight because I didn't want to disappoint the marketing team. In my current role, I've learnt about the importance of office politics. I've observed plenty of occasions when people's ideas have been shot down not because they were bad ideas, but because the people suggesting them were insufficiently friendly with the managing director.

When you ask whether the interviewers are more interested in the skills you acquired or the lessons you learned, they can easily say *Both*! So be ready to give a full response to the question.

Why did you leave each previous employer?

If the interviewers are asking you this question, then they may have a concern that you are the kind of person who flits from one company to the next. If the company were to offer you a job, are you likely to join them for good or get bored and move on after only a couple of months? The interviewers may have this concern if they read on your CV that you've had a number of jobs but stayed in each of them for less than 18 months or so.

In reality, people leave one company to join another for all sorts of reasons. But some reasons are more acceptable in the eyes of interviewers than others. Try to focus on the positive reasons that led you to move to a new company rather than dwell overly on the negative aspects of the job that made you want to leave your last one.

Some of the most acceptable reasons for leaving include:

- **Seeking greater responsibility**: *I enjoyed my time there, but after only a year, the other teachers were telling me what a fantastic job I was doing and that they wished I was head of department. Unfortunately the incumbent was showing no signs of wanting to leave, so I realised I would need to find a new school if I wanted to progress.*

- **Wanting more of a challenge**: *I was managing a number of mid-sized accounts at that company and quickly got to grips with the role. Within a year, I realised that I was ready for more of a challenge to keep me interested and on my toes, so I moved companies. I'm still managing similarly-sized accounts, but they tend to be more complex in nature.*

- **Searching for greater security**: *I had joined that business believing it was a stable place to work. Unfortunately it went through a couple of rounds of redundancy and I didn't feel that it was offering me an environment in which I could do my best work, so I was looking to join a more established and stable company.*

- **Seeking full-time employment**: *I was originally hired to provide maternity cover for six months. The other executive decided to take another three months off and was willing to do a job share with me when she returned, but I'm now looking for a full-time job in which I can fully immerse myself.*

- **Wanting to develop yourself**: *My goal has always been to move into general management. In my previous roles I was getting a lot of experience of managing the cost side of the equation, but I was lacking the experience of managing the revenue side. So I deliberately sought out a move into sales and marketing by joining that next company.*

Finish off with a statement to assure the interviewers that you are now ready to settle down into a career with a single employer:

I realise that I have moved around a couple of times in my career already. But all those moves have helped me to develop particular skills. I am now ready to stay with one employer so long as they are able to offer me good development opportunities.

Are you a good manager?

I'm sure you realise that answering anything other than 'yes' to this question is foolish if you're applying for a managerial role. But rather than just saying 'yes', make sure you explain in a couple of sentences why you think you're a good manager.

For example, you can mention three or four of the key skills that you exercise as a manager. The following list may help you:

- ✔ Delegating work, supervising it, and checking for mistakes.
- ✔ Coaching, developing, or mentoring members of your team.
- ✔ Creating a vision or business strategy for your department or business unit.
- ✔ Working with the management team or board on issues affecting the whole organisation.
- ✔ Inspiring or motivating your team to achieve results.
- ✔ Shaping the atmosphere or culture within your team or department.

Vary the extent to which you talk up your experience and skill in the job depending on the seniority of the role and the responsibility that goes with it.

For a very senior role, focus on the more strategic side of management:

Yes, I think that my team would say that I am a good manager. Having such a large team, I rely on my direct reports to manage the department on a day-to-day basis. My role is to coach my direct reports and hopefully help them to progress to larger roles elsewhere in the business. The majority of my time is spent interfacing with other departments and working with the rest of the management team on the strategic management of the overall business.

If you have only had limited supervisory experience, give a more measured response:

Yes, I'm a good manager because I try to understand what the members of my team are good or not so good at. That understanding allows me to delegate work that plays to each individual's strengths.

Sidestepping Questions about Your Current Company

Interviewers can be quite nosy; they often like to have a poke around and find out a bit about the company that you are (or have been) working for. Just as the presenter Loyd Grossman used to ask in that TV programme *Through the Keyhole* 'What kind of a person lives in a house like this?', the interviewers want to understand 'What kind of a person works in a company like this?'.

How you talk about your current company often reflects on what the interviewers think of you. No company is perfect, but if you bad-mouth your current employer too much, the interviewers may start to wonder if it really is such a terrible place to work – or is it just that you are a terribly negative person or a person who is terribly difficult to please?

Exercise discretion when talking about your current employer, especially if the company by which you are being interviewed is a competitor to your current company. Giving away confidential information not only can land you in hot water with your current employer, but also raises concerns in the interviewers' minds that you may one day be equally disloyal in a future job interview when talking about their company.

How would you describe your current company?

While bad-mouthing your current company too much makes you sound like a terminally miserable individual, talking in overly glowing terms about the company simply won't ring true either. If your current company really is such a fantastic place to work, why are you leaving?

 Try to mention twice as many good points as bad points when describing your current employer. And finish off your response by referring to specific aspects of the interviewers' organisation that you find attractive.

Here are some examples of responses that meet the two-thirds to one-third rule:

✔ *It's a good place to work. The directors are very transparent in their decision making, so we all feel very involved in the direction of the company and the decisions that are made. We also have quite a cohesive team so we're friends as well as colleagues and we make the effort to go out for lunch or a drink a couple of times a month. The only down side is that the company hasn't grown much in the last couple of years, which means that there has been almost no opportunity for promotion. And that's the main reason that I'm looking to join a growing business such as yours.*

✔ *The company is growing fairly quickly and as such it's an exciting place to work because we have so many new projects to work on. The company prides itself on its culture of focusing on results rather than how we work. So we dress casually in the office and the managers let us work from home as often as we like so long as it doesn't affect our ability to do the work. The only reason I'm looking to leave is because the company has a policy that means that I can't transfer from my current role into an account executive role. Obviously, your company is rather more progressive in that respect, which brings me here today.*

How would you rate your current boss?

Although you may get away with pointing out negative aspects of your current company, you'll be treading on far more danger-ous ground in disparaging your boss. In any situation involving differences of opinion, two sides exist to the story. By talking about the failings of your current boss, the interviewers may wonder if some of the fault actually lies with you.

Always be positive about your current manager's abilities, and keep any sinister thoughts to yourself!

> ✔ *I have a good boss at the moment. He gives me a lot of lati-tude in how I do my work. We meet for a couple of hours about once a week to tackle any problems that I raise. And he trusts me completely, so it's refreshing not to be micro-managed at all. All in all, he's a good manager to work for.*

> ✔ *I would rate my boss quite highly. I think that she has really taken the time to understand what I want out of my career and has given tasks that help me to achieve my goal of moving into a customer-facing role. And she was very understanding when my son was involved in a car accident last year and I needed to take quite a few days off to help with his convalescence.*

 Don't make your current boss sound *too* fantastic. If one of the interviewers is your prospective future boss, they may start to feel insecure!

What's your boss's biggest failing?

If the interviewers specifically ask you to criticise your boss, try to deflect the question by emphasising only their good qualities.

To be honest, I don't think my manager has any major failings. She has a lot of experience in the field so I'm always surprised by how much I keep learning from her. And she has a very dry sense of humour that makes her good fun to be around.

If the interviewers continue to push you to point out a failing or fault in your current boss, then allow yourself to point out some relatively minor issues.

> ✔ *I still find it difficult to think of anything that's a real failing. I suppose this is more of a minor quibble. My manager tends to be incredibly busy and spends quite a lot of time out of the office, which means that it can be quite difficult to get paperwork signed off when I need to get authorisation to spend on a large item. But I really don't want to blow it out of all proportion as he has lots of good points that I've already mentioned.*

> ✔ *It's really difficult to think of much to complain about. But if I'm being really picky I guess he can be a bit forgetful at times. He's forgotten times and dates of meetings on a couple of occasions. But it doesn't happen often and nowadays I always take the precaution of copying e-mails in to his personal assistant so that she can discretely manage his schedule.*

Why do you want to leave your current company?

Just as you need to emphasise the positive qualities of jobs that you moved to when answering *Why did you leave each previous employer?* (refer to this section earlier in the chapter for tackling that question), you need to avoid whingeing about the negative aspects of your current employment situation such as dull colleagues or a hopeless boss. Focus instead on the positive qualities of the company that is interviewing you.

It's not that I want to leave my current company so much as wanting to join yours. I enjoy my current work and have some great colleagues and I'm sure that I'll keep in touch with quite a few of them after I leave. But what I hope to gain from joining your organisation is the greater involvement in international projects that I've not had so far in my career.

What is your current notice period?

This is a mostly factual question. Read your employment contract before the interview to ensure that you give the right answer and don't raise a potential employer's hopes by telling them your notice period is only a month if you are really tied in for three months!

Don't forget to take into account any leave days that you may have accrued. If the employer is looking to fill a vacancy urgently, then being able to join even a few days earlier may swing the decision in your favour. On the other hand, if you do have any holidays planned that you are unwilling to change, do mention them.

My notice period is four weeks. But I have five days' annual leave that I have yet to take. So in theory I could hand in my notice and start with a new company within three weeks.

In a few very competitive industries and certain highly-paid jobs, employers sometimes put employees on *gardening leave* when they give notice. The employers no longer want the employees in their workplace (possibly building up ideas or contacts to take to a new job) so they send them on a period of paid absence. Do mention if this may be the case for you.

Technically, my contract says that I have to give three months' notice. But when other analysts have handed in their notice in our department, the bank has always just paid them off and asked them to leave immediately. The only slight wrinkle is that I have just arranged to take my kids to Disneyland in two weeks' time, so I wouldn't be able to start until I return in three weeks.

May we approach your referees?

Consider asking interviewers to hold off from checking your references until you have received a definite offer of a job. You don't want to irritate your referees by bombarding them with requests for references from too many companies.

If you are still in employment and any of your referees work at your company, you may be worried about the prospect of alerting them to the fact that you're looking for a job. If you explain your situation in the following way, you'll probably find that most interviewers are very understanding:

I'd be happy for you to check my references eventually and I'm sure that they will confirm everything that I've been saying about myself in this interview. But would you mind waiting until you've decided to make me a firm offer? I'd rather not draw their attention to the fact that I'm looking elsewhere for a job.

If you have already left an employer, then your answer can be an unmitigated yes:

Please do approach my referees. The contact details for my last boss and the operations director are at the bottom of my CV. I'm sure that they will say pretty much the same thing about me as I've been telling you.

Most employers make job offers contingent on receiving satisfactory references. So when you receive such an offer, talk to your referee to make sure that what you have told your new employer corresponds with what your referee is going to tell them.

Chapter 7

Talking about Why You Want a New Job

*I*nterviewers understandably want to find out why you want to work in their industry and, more specifically, why you want to work for them as opposed to one of their competitors.

In this chapter, I give you advice on how to impress interviewers with your knowledge of their company and how to talk about what you are looking for in your new job with them.

Answering Questions about the Employer

When employers are looking for the perfect person for the job, they often comment that a lot of candidates tend to have fairly similar skills and experience. So interviewers ask questions to figure out how much you know about their organisation and the job on offer. After all, if someone were applying to work with you, wouldn't you want to know why?

Make sure to visit the interviewing company's Web site and read all the literature available to you about the company and the role. And if the organisation is a big one, check the

Financial Times or the business sections of quality national newspapers to see if any recent developments have hit the headlines.

If the company has branches, showrooms, restaurants, or shops, visit them at least a couple of times to get a feel for the company – interviewers take a dim view of candidates who don't.

What do you know about our company?

While this is a very open-ended question, treat it as if the interviewers have asked you to repeat back to them a couple of positive points attracting you to the company. Even if you have come across some information about a crisis or failure in the company, avoid mentioning it unless the interviewers specifically ask you about it.

Engage in some subtle flattery about the interviewers' company. The interviewers probably enjoy working there, and they want to know that you will too. Slip in some mentions of how you know what you know about the company: Good phrases include *I saw on your Web site*, *I read in the Financial Times*, *I gathered from your annual report*, and so on.

Take a look at these example responses:

✔ *I know that you are a growing organisation with a turnover of around £70 million last year and that you were awarded the Chemical Engineering Federation's Award for Innovation two years ago. I read in your annual report that you are increasingly moving into injection moulded plastics, which I believe will be a growth area given the trend for car manufacturers to use it in their assembly processes.*

✔ *I've been living in the area for a few years now and used to go into your restaurant on the high street. I have always been impressed by the quality of the food and the fact that the menu changes every month to incorporate produce that is in season. The waiting staff has without exception been attentive and friendly too. So when I heard that you were opening another restaurant and were recruiting, it was really a no-brainer to apply to work for you.*

> ✔ *I used to work as an in-house lawyer and our head of department always used to say that if she had the budget, she would be using your firm. I read on your Web site that you have recently opened an office in Amsterdam and are opening another early next year in Prague in line with the managing partner's vision of creating a truly European firm. And if I'm honest, that kind of growth and opportunity is very attractive.*

> ✔ *I appreciate the fact that you use only organic, natural ingredients in your skincare products. I also read on your Web site that you have ambitious growth plans and that the board is unwilling to sell out to a large multinational business because they are worried that they may dilute the original philosophy of the company's founders to use natural ingredients and recipes that have been handed down the generations.*

Don't think that you can get away without doing your research just because a company is not a large business that gets discussed in the newspapers. Just about every company has some kind of brochure that they send out to customers interested in their services or products. If applying for a job, ring up and be honest – tell them that you have an interview with them and ask if it's okay to get some of their materials.

How much do you know about this position?

Before you go for the interview, practise saying out loud the key responsibilities of the job. This is a critically important question and you do not want to have to utter any *erms* or *ums* when answering it.

Try these responses on for size:

> ✔ *I gather that it is a full-time position working in either the Fulham or Ealing health clubs. The main responsibility is educating gym users and ensuring that they are using the equipment safely. And if they want a personal training plan, to sit down with them, understand their goals, and structure a workout schedule for them. At the same time, the job's not just about safety and training but also about building a rapport with gym users so that they grow accustomed to visiting the gym and are therefore more likely to renew their memberships when they expire.*

> ✔ *The successful applicant will work directly with the pur-*
> *chasing director. The biggest part of the role will be to pro-*
> *vide administrative support to the director as well as the*
> *two purchasing managers, which may include anything*
> *from arranging travel and overnight stays for them to han-*
> *dling incoming phone calls and formatting the occasional*
> *document.*

Many organisations send out a job description if you ask for it.
Or a job description may be downloadable from the jobs section of their Web site. Even if the organisation does not provide
you with a full job description, read the job advert thoroughly
to ensure that you memorise the main responsibilities and
duties associated with the job. If applying for a job through a
recruitment agency, make sure you get as much detailed information from the agency about the job as possible.

How would you rate our products / services / Web site?

Don't automatically assume that you must flatter the interviewers by making implausibly positive remarks about their
products, services, or Web site. If the fact that these aspects
are flawed or missing some key element in some way is
common knowledge, then the interviewers may appreciate
your insight.

Use the *2:1 rule* when discussing the company's products and
services. Doing so means making at least two positive comments about the company's product before mentioning one
negative comment. For example:

I think your clothing range is fantastic – otherwise I wouldn't be
applying to work here. The women's basics are extremely good
value and it always surprises me how quickly you get catwalk
trends into your shops. The smarter clothes are also very
impressive – I've spotted that a few other shops on the high
street are following your lead in having a more tailored jacket
shape this season. I guess the only gap is a men's range, but I've
read rumours in the trade press that you are thinking of launch-
ing one next year.

Do your research before the interview in order to answer this question successfully. If the company has a tangible product, get your hands on it beforehand so that you can experience it for yourself.

If applying for a role involving you using or selling the company's products or services, make sure that you are extremely familiar with them. If applying for a support role – for example in finance, human resources, or the legal team –you can get away with a more passing familiarity with the products or services.

What is it that attracts you to our company?

This question is very similar to *What do you know about our company?* (detailed earlier in this chapter). Think about how the organisation likes to portray itself to the outside world and answer this question by listing two or three qualities or characteristics that attract you to it, specifically explaining why each of those qualities are of interest to you.

> ✔ *You have a great reputation in the marketplace and it's extremely important for me to be working for a market leader. Your two-month training programme would be an excellent springboard for my career, too.*

> ✔ *The school has an excellent reputation in the county for helping its students to achieve top exam grades. You also have some of the best facilities and resources. More than that, I've been very impressed by some of the other teachers that I met last week – they all seemed relaxed, friendly, and very supportive.*

To really impress the interviewers, have a few more qualities or characteristics up your sleeve that attract you to the company. When you have told the interviewers your top two or three reasons, state: *I could go on with more reasons if you would like?*

Ramping up for a revamp

If you're being hired to revamp part of the company – for example, the role is specifically to do with turning around the business – then feel free to constructively criticise the company.

I think the products used to be leaders in the field about three or four years ago. But some of the discount retailers have really brought the quality of their products up to scratch, which has left some of your products looking a little tired. But the situation's not irrecoverable as I think customers still have a great affinity for the brand.

How would you rate us against our competitors?

Most interviewers want to hear that they rate very highly against their competitors. Of course, this question assumes that you know not only quite a bit about the interviewers' company but also have at least a passing familiarity with their main competitors.

Talk up some of the positive ways in which this company compares with its competitors. Even if the company is not the largest, it may be the fastest growing. Perhaps the company has some highly rated products or the best training programme. Just make sure you have something positive to say!

You have a fantastic reputation. You grew by 9 per cent last year, which was nearly twice that of any other publisher. And you're the market leader in the health and fitness and youth magazine segments, which are both predicted to be major growth areas in the medium term.

What do you think our unique selling point is?

Most organisations believe that they are better than their competitors or unique in some respect. A *unique selling point* is pretty much what it says – the reason why a company stands out as different to its competitors. If asked this question, tell the interviewers what they want to hear.

I believe you're still the only company that produces its drinks using only entirely fresh ingredients, while all of the other fruit drink makers use at least some fruit from concentrate.

Your research (refer to Chapter 2) should uncover some hints as to how the company sees itself. Look for how the company describes itself and try to paraphrase some of these back at the interviewers.

Even if you can't unearth any features that are entirely unique to this one organisation, you can argue that the combination of two or three aspects makes it unique.

Your bank offers some of the best value products on the high street while at the same time offering customers the ability to ring up their local branch rather than be put through to a faceless call centre.

Do you have any concerns about our organisation?

Even if you do have some concerns, your safest bet is to keep these to yourself for the moment. Wait until you have been offered a job to ask the questions that you really want answered. If asked this question during the initial interview, use the opportunity to reiterate one or two reasons why you want to work for this company:

Not at all. I like what I've seen and heard so far. In particular, I didn't realise that the fast-track promotion scheme was being made available to all of the team leaders. So that would be a real bonus for me.

The only exception to this rule would be if some piece of news or a rumour has been widely reported in the trade press or newspapers:

Nearly everything does sound great about your company. But I have to say that the recent departure of your finance director and the subsequent drop in your share price did leave me wondering about the financial stability of the business. Rumour has it that you will need to make mass redundancies to achieve your end-of-year target. How may that affect the team that I would be joining?

If you were in charge of our company, what would you do differently?

This question tends to be asked of managerial rather than entry-level candidates, and isn't a question to regularly expect to come up against. But the way to answer this really tough question successfully is to compliment the company and then to offer only limited and constructive criticism. Don't take this question as an invitation to pass judgement on how poorly the whole organisation is run! And don't just say *nothing* when asked if you'd run anything differently within the company. The interviewers are looking for an intelligent opinion rather than outright flattery.

Answering Questions about What You're Looking For

Interviewers almost always want to know why you are looking to leave your current employer and why you may want to join their organisation. You should also be ready to answer questions about what you are looking for and what other companies you may be applying to.

Why are you looking to leave your current company?

This question is very similar to *Why did you leave each previous company?* (covered in Chapter 6).

You win more brownie points by talking about why you want to join the interviewers' organisation than by whingeing about what is wrong with your current employer.

Try one of these sample answers on for size:

> ✔ *I don't really want to leave as I've got some good friends there. But I think that I have learned as much as I can. In order to push myself, I need to work for a larger business that will offer me a greater diversity of personnel and training issues.*

> ✔ *The situation is not so much that I want to leave my current hospital as I want to join your department. In order to reach my goal of becoming a certified physiotherapist, I need to get more experience of working with patients with sports injuries, which I would be able to get with you.*

If your current job isn't challenging you, what could you do to change it?

So many candidates talk about wanting to move jobs because their current one 'isn't challenging enough' that this reason has become a bit of a cliché. In asking this question, the interviewers want to know if you simply moan about not being challenged enough in your current job or whether you ever try to change the nature of your role.

The ideal response is to state that you tried to pursue more interesting work but found that the organisation's rules or perhaps your boss would not let you.

I did ask my boss if I could sit in on more of the production team's meetings and he was receptive to the idea. But HR said that some of the production team may take offence because they are a higher grade than I am, so they asked me to stop attending. I thought it was fairly outrageous, but that's the company's policy.

Don't lie! If you never took any action to try to change your current job, then don't say that you did. Instead, try an answer like this one:

I suppose I could ask my boss if I could transfer into the compliance team. I haven't to date because my boss has been under a lot of pressure recently, as the team has been one member short. I thought that I should wait until they filled the vacancy, but to be honest six months have passed and there's still no sign of the position being filled.

Why do you want to work in this industry?

Before you blurt out the real reasons why you want to work in the interviewers' industry, do think about the socially acceptable reasons for doing so. For example, saying that you want to work in television production because *It sounds glamorous and well paid* won't go down as well as saying *Every day is different and you have an instrumental role in communicating interesting ideas to a wide audience.*

Respond to this question by emphasising your skills and strengths. Here's another example to base your own on:

I've always wanted to work in the not-for-profit sector because I feel that it's important to be giving something back to the community and society as a whole rather than only making profit for shareholders. The people that I've talked to so far all seem to have a real desire and passion to make a difference, and I really want to be surrounded by people like that rather than people who work only to earn a living.

If moving from one industry into a new one, have two or three reasons why you are making the move. You may want to compare and contrast your old industry with your new one, too.

In the insurance sector, people tend to be pigeonholed depending on what they've done before. From my reading and discussions with people in the consumer goods sector, I get the impression that a lot more flexibility exists in how teams work together and the way that people are allowed to carve out their own careers depending on where they want to go in the future.

Who else are you applying to?

In the dim and distant past, applying to multiple employers may have been taken as a sign of disloyalty. But in today's job market, responding that you have applied to a number of companies shouldn't be a problem. You want your response to indicate that you are actively looking – but you don't necessarily need to name the other employers or go into specifics.

Feel free to say that you have applied for the same role in different companies. But saying that you have applied for many different roles is almost certain to be read as a sign of indecision about what you really want from your career.

See if you can adapt one of these example answers to suit your situation:

> ✔ *I've applied to the other large accountancy firms as well. I've decided that I want to train as an auditor, but I want to work for a nationwide firm rather than a local or even medium-sized firm.*

> ✔ *I've applied to a range of companies who are all willing to support employees in achieving the national certificate in IT skills. I've applied to a couple of businesses in the Bromley area as well as the local council. But I have to say that my preference would be to work for a small company such as yours where I could get to know the rest of the team.*

How does this job compare with others you're looking at?

This question is often an obvious follow up to *Who else are you applying to?* (dealt with in the previous section). A good answer must explain to the interviewers why you think that this job is better than the others you're considering. Draw upon your research on the company's nature and offerings for an ideal response (refer to Chapter 2 for more on research).

In reality, the differences between competitors in the same sector may be very slight to people outside of that industry. But you can bet that those differences seem very pronounced to those who work in that industry, so make sure that you understand them.

Have a look at these good responses:

> ✔ *It's difficult to distinguish between the different jobs because this is the first interview that I have attended. But you have been very friendly yet challenging today. And the fact that your recruitment team responded so quickly probably says something about the efficiency and professionalism of the rest of the organisation, too.*

> ✔ *The day-to-day job isn't in itself that different from the other hospitality jobs. What is different, though, is that you are a part of a much larger group, which would give me greater options for career progression in the medium-to-long term.*

> ✔ *Given that you won a national award for your graduate training scheme last year, I'd be silly to want to work anywhere else.*

Have you received any job offers so far?

Interviewers often think that candidates who have received job offers from elsewhere – particularly from their competitors – are probably more desirable than ones who have not. The ideal response talks about other offers that you have received.

Yes, I've received an offer from Alliance Ventures for the same role. But my gut instinct is that the culture here would suit me much more. While the people here obviously work hard, I get the feeling that you don't take yourselves quite so seriously as they do at Alliance.

Don't lie if you haven't received any offers, though! If the interviewers start to ask more questions about your other offers, you'll almost certainly get caught out! If you haven't received any offers, just be honest and say that you have yet to receive any.

No, I haven't yet. But this is only the second interview that I have attended so far and I have at least two more interviews in the next few weeks.

How would you describe your dream job?

This is a trick question. The interviewers are surreptitiously trying to sound out how much you want to work in the position that is on offer. The interviewers will reject you if you describe a job that is too far removed from what is on offer. Respond to this question by mentioning as many positive aspects of this job as you can.

Think about the specific job you're applying for. What are the positive aspects of this job that make you want to work for this company?

> ✔ *I've always wanted to work in sales. I enjoy the process of researching customers and pursuing them until I can close a deal. I can't really imagine working in any other function.*
>
> ✔ *My long-term, dream job is to become a finance manager. So what I hope to get out of this job is a solid training, plus support and sponsorship for me to complete my accountancy exams.*
>
> ✔ *What I'm looking for is a job that will provide me with some career opportunities. I've had a couple of jobs in the last few years, but I want to settle down with one company that will provide me with good training and hopefully opportunities to develop myself.*

Don't talk about your fantasy job – perhaps transatlantic journeys in first class, mingling with celebrities, and earning pots of cash for very little work (admit it . . . you want to be a footballer). Talk about realistic aspects of your 'dream' job, such as good training, promotion prospects, a sociable team, and so on.

Who would your ideal employer be?

Be careful of this trick question. You can get into hot water if you name an organisation too different from the one interviewing you. The interviewers obviously want to hire someone who wants to work for them; they won't want to hire someone who is considering their organisation only as a second choice. However, don't lie. Unless the interviewers' organisation genuinely is your ideal employer, don't say that it is. Instead, focus on some of the attributes about this organisation that do attract you.

Consider these two answers:

> ✔ *I want to work for a large employer that is truly international in scope. Getting a good training programme is obviously very important. And I want the opportunity further down the line – perhaps three or five years in the future – to be able to transfer to an overseas office.*

> ✔ *My ideal employer would be based in the Oxford area. It would be a small firm of surveyors because I want to get to know a team well. And it would specialise in commercial and industrial rather than residential projects because that is where my interest lies. So your firm fits all three of those criteria for me.*

Evaluating Your Fit With the Organisation

Candidates often have unrealistic expectations that the grass really will be greener on the other side of the fence. However, interviewers know that the upside of moving to their company may also be accompanied by possible downsides such as minor problems readjusting to new team mates and a new culture – and what they want to know is whether you realise that too.

What do you think you can bring to the team?

Treat this question as if the interviewer is asking you to name two or three skills and qualities that they want and you have. Make sure that you tailor your response to how you would use those skills and qualities in the team environment.

Even if you have already answered questions about your skills and experience, interviewers rarely tire of hearing the same message.

> ✔ *What I can bring to the team begins with my research credentials and track record of adding value through both qualitative and quantitative research. I'm also the sort of person who doesn't give up easily when faced with a challenge. In fact, I positively enjoy having new problems to crack. All in all, I think I'd be a real asset to the team.*

> ✔ *I've been told that I'm a good person to have on the team because I'm willing to give of myself. I actively enjoy coaching and enthusing others about the work because it's a job that I'm enormously passionate about.*

If the interviewers want you to talk in more detail about what you can bring to their company, think back to some of the answers you have prepared in response to questions asking you to talk about yourself (refer to Chapter 4).

We are a diverse company – how will you cope with that?

By *diversity*, employers are usually referring to the fact that their company encourages employees regardless of their gender, age, race, religion, or sexual orientation. A good answer is to say that you would have no problem with this situation because your current employer is also very diverse.

I'm glad to hear that your company is very diverse because our company is too. Thinking about our department alone, we have more female managers than male managers. The department head is ten years younger than I am. And I'm pretty sure that most minorities and other cultures are very well represented too.

If you have not worked in a very diverse company, you can try to argue that you would very much like to join this particular company precisely because of its diversity.

Your company's diversity is one of the factors that leads me to want to work for you. I have to admit that our small company does tend to be a bit white, middle class, and male and I think that's a real shame as we probably don't employ the best talent that we could.

What kind of manager would you like to work for?

The interviewers want to see how you may fit into their particular organisation, so no single 'right' answer applies to all interviewers. You need to figure out the kind of culture and style of manager that you may end up with in this company.

Consider these two example responses:

✔ *I'd like to work for a manager who is supportive of me and my career goals. I've reached the stage now where I'm good at my job but I want to advance to the next level. So I hope that my manager will be brave enough to give me big projects and challenging work that keep me interested.*

✔ *I enjoy working for supervisors who are very clear in communicating exactly what they want from the rest of the team. I've observed teams having problems when it hasn't been clear who was supposed to be doing what.*

How long do you plan to stay in this job?

One of the biggest concerns employers have is recruiting a candidate who decides to leave after only a handful of months. Especially if an employer is planning to invest time and money in training you, they probably want you to stay for a period of at least three or four years. Make it clear that you are looking to develop your career within a single organisation – theirs.

Saying that you want to change roles in less than a couple of years is okay so long as you make it clear that you want to stay with the one employer.

I can see myself staying with you for the foreseeable future – certainly for at least three or five years. As I've explained though, I don't see myself staying in the role of internal compliance for more than nine months to a year. I see it as a stepping stone to achieving a regional management position either in the UK or the rest of Europe.

If you've jumped around a lot of jobs, try to reassure the interviewers that you are now looking for career stability. Perhaps mitigating circumstances (such as family circumstances) led to you changing jobs in the past. So be sure to set the interviewers' minds at ease that, should you be offered the job, you will not leave within just a few months.

Why should we hire you?

This question sounds quite intimidating and the interviewers can often sound as if they doubt your ability. But answering this question successfully only requires you to summarise the most important skills and qualities that you have and the employer is looking for.

I have already mentioned the skills that I believe I have in terms of growing existing accounts and winning new ones. I also have an extensive network of contacts throughout the industry, which allows me to keep abreast of ideas and developments in the field. In addition to that, I'm determined to become a partner in a business within the next 18 months so you know that I'll be dedicated and hard working in order to achieve that.

Where do you see yourself in five years' time?

I have heard so many candidates stumble at this hurdle because they have not prepared an answer to it! The truth is that you probably don't know what you want to be doing in five years' time – but you can't say that to interviewers as they may take it as a sign of lack of forethought.

Five years is conceivably long enough to say that you want to be doing something outside of the company – such as setting up your own business. But the safer bet is to say that you are looking for some form of career progression within the company.

Given that your company has just announced plans to open a third office in the Oxfordshire region, I assume that there will be opportunities for progression within the business. Within a couple of years I hope to be promoted to an assistant merchan-diser and then sometime after that to a merchandising manager. So I could easily see myself working for you in five or even more years' time.

When would you be available to start?

Don't count your chickens before they're hatched! The interviewers are not necessarily saying that they want you to start with them immediately. Treat this question as if the interviewers are asking you about your notice period (see Chapter 6).

Deflecting Questions about Money

People don't like to talk about money. Just as most people think asking their mates how much they're earning is a bit rude, interviewers and candidates tend to skirt around the issue too.

A lot of employers give an indication of the salary on offer in their job advert. But plenty of employers try to attract as many candidates as possible with vague statements such as 'competitive salary' or 'highly attractive package'.

The golden rule is to delay talking about money for as long as you can. In the early rounds of the interview process, the balance of power lies with the interviewers. But once the interviewers have made you an offer, the balance of power swings in your favour – only then try to negotiate over pay.

How much are you earning at the moment?

This is a fairly straightforward factual question. Answer the question by telling the interviewers exactly how much you are currently earning.

Don't price yourself out of the market by implying the interviewer must automatically match your salary. You may want so say something like: *My salary is only one part of the equation. What is most important to me is finding the right role that will challenge and develop me.* You may currently be earning more than the interviewers are expecting to pay, but they may conceivably raise their offer if you're the right person for the job.

Bear in mind the relative scarcity in the market of people with your skills and experience. For example, fewer executives with ten years' experience of running an advertising agency are out there than advertising trainees with only a year's experience. The more certain you are that your skills are in short supply, the more bullish you can probably afford to be with your answers.

Consider the following two example responses:

- *I'm earning £18,500 with up to a 10 per cent bonus plus benefits at the moment. However, as I said earlier, I'm more interested in finding the right organisation that will help me to achieve my long-term career goal of becoming a store manager than earning a few pounds more at this moment in time.*

- *My basic salary is £85,000 and I'm entitled to a bonus and profit share, which could be as much as £40,000 this year. But I'd rather not get bogged down in talk about money because I think we should probably spend this initial discussion establishing whether I'm the right candidate to turn around your business.*

How important is money to you?

Most employers like to believe that they hire people who would continue to work for them even if they won the Lottery.

Consider these two good responses:

- *Of course I need to earn enough to live on, but money isn't a major factor in deciding where I should work. It's more important for me to work for a business that has a solid reputation and good prospects for development and progression.*

- *Money isn't important in its own right. It's more important to me that I'm doing a good job and receiving recognition for my hard work and achievements. I suppose that my salary and bonus are financial indicators of how well the business thinks I'm doing. If I'm doing a good job, I want the business to recognise that by awarding me a fair bonus.*

The main exception to the rule is sales people, employers of whom are sometimes sceptical of candidates who do not think that money is terribly important. Below is a good response for this situation:

I must admit that I want the things in life that money can buy – such as a big house, a plasma television, a fantastic car, and two or three holidays a year. But I realise that you don't get anything for nothing, so I'm prepared to work incredibly hard to get what I want out of life.

How much do you think you are worth in a job?

If the organisation has yet to make you a firm offer, resist the temptation to reply to this question with too specific a number. Your best bet is to dodge the question by saying that finding the right job and organisation to work for is more important than getting a big wad of cash (even if that isn't necessarily true!).

Read up on job adverts and talk to headhunters, recruitment agencies, and other people in your profession and industry to get a rough idea of your worth in case the interviewers press you for a more specific figure.

Having looked at other similar opportunities, it seems that managers with my kind of background and experience are being made offers in the region of £30,000 to £35,000. But, as I said earlier, my primary consideration is finding the right company to join.

What would you consider adequate remuneration for this role?

Even though the question sounds like a request for a precise number, the same rule applies as for any other question regarding pay: Unless you have already received a firm offer, avoid pricing yourself out of the market by stating a number that may be too high for the company to afford.

Avoid the tawdry topic of money by reiterating that finding a job that allows you to develop your skills and further your career ambitions is your primary goal.

Obviously I'm looking for more than I am currently earning. But that's not the only factor that will decide my next career move. I'm more anxious to ensure that I feel I can add real value and that the management team will take my ideas and opinions seriously.

Sales people are the exception to the rule. Sales people are typically very motivated by money and interviewers expect sales people to want to talk about money.

At the moment I'm on a basic salary of £12,000. For the first £100,000 of sales that I generate, I earn a 6 per cent commission. For anything over that, I earn 8 per cent commission. So I'd need an offer that could beat that.

I'm afraid you're a bit expensive for us

Perhaps you've told the interviewers exactly how much you are earning and they reply with this statement. Don't be despondent, however. Employers usually have some discretion to offer a bigger pay package for the right candidate. Don't give the interviewers a disgusted look and abandon the interview. Do your best to convince the interviewers that you are the strongest candidate. And once they have selected you over all the other candidates, you may find that they can boost the overall offer.

Even though an employer may not be able to beat what you are currently earning, try negotiating a deal that is better for you in the medium-to-long term. For example, you may be able to ask for a deferred pay rise, share options, or a bonus based on performance.

Just because I earn a little bit more than you are currently willing to pay doesn't mean that I'm no longer interested in this opportunity. I'm intrigued to find out more about why this vacancy has arisen, and perhaps we can work something out if I am the right candidate for you.

What would you like to be earning in two years' time?

If you answer with too high a number, the interviewers may think that you have unrealistic expectations about the job. But if you answer with too low a number, you may unwittingly commit yourself to receiving unreasonably low pay rises for the foreseeable future!

Try to avoid answering with numbers at all. Focus on what you want in terms of career progression and job satisfaction.

I'd like to be earning more, but the precise number isn't that crucial to me. My primary aim is to progress in my career. My understanding from your Web site is that good assistant managers can feasibly be promoted to general managers within 18 months to two years.

Interviewers can ask you about every conceivable time frame. So be ready to talk about how much you may want to be earning (and where you want to be in terms of career progression and job satisfaction) in three, four, five, and more years.

Four years is quite a long time away, but I hope to have made significant progress in my career and be on course to becoming a fully-fledged resort manager. I really don't have that much of an idea of the earning potential as I'm much more focused on furthering my skills and getting international work experience under my belt.

Chapter 8

Thriving Under the Pressure Interview

. . . .

In This Chapter

▶ Getting to grips with pressure interviewing

▶ Keeping calm in the face of an interview onslaught

▶ Working out answers to common pressure questions

▶ Handling other odd questions

▶ Coming up with something to say to any question

. . . .

*A*ll interviewers can be mean. But certain interviewers take their meanness even further, subscribing to a school of interviewing that believes that candidates should be put under extreme pressure to see how the candidate fares. These guys really want to make you squirm.

Interviewers with this outlook see it as a way of testing how you may cope with unexpected situations and stress on the job. What would you do if you went to a meeting with an unhappy customer screaming abuse at you? What if a colleague burst into your office saying that a warehouse fire has destroyed all your stock? Or what if aliens have abducted half of the team but you still need to get the project completed by midday? Okay, the latter isn't terribly likely to happen. But you get the idea – these interviewers want to see whether you would crack under the strain or cope with confidence.

The problem with pressure interviewers is, you never know when you may meet one. These people look just like any other interviewers and they may even start off being all smiley and ask you some nice easy questions. Suddenly the questions and the tone of the interview may change. This chapter is about preparing for the commonest pressure questions. And because you can never prepare for every single question that you're likely to be asked, I finish off by discussing some ways to deflect all manner of odd and uncomfortable questions.

Maintaining Your Composure

Pressure interviewing is designed to throw you off balance. The interviewer may hope that the sheer strangeness of the question puts you at a loss for words. Or the interviewer may pose a very straightforward question but ask it in a decidedly negative or condescending tone in the hopes of eliciting some kind of emotional reaction – perhaps a moment of hesitation and indecision, or a touch of annoyance. The key to dealing with pressure interviewing is to always keep calm. *Who would you rather meet – Albert Einstein or Michael Jackson?* Well, in response to this question, I'd be tempted to quip back *Michael Jackson because Einstein's corpse would probably smell quite badly.* But being flippant in an interview will win you no points. Even if the question sounds completely ridiculous – which many of them are – you must follow the interviewer's lead and answer it as if it were a perfectly natural question.

Another common tactic used by pressure interviewers is to make negative statements about you and see how you react. The interviewers may shake their heads and say: *I just don't think you're emotionally tough enough for the job.* Now, some candidates may sit there and think, oh well, that's my chance gone. But a good candidate in this situation shows their backbone by asking, *Why do you think that?* or perhaps *I'm surprised you say that. I know that I'm tough enough and I'll give you an example of when I demonstrated my emotional toughness. . .*

No matter how stupid or odd a question or statement, don't let your puzzlement or irritation show. Keep a neutral expression on your face at all times. Perhaps nod sagely as you think about the answer, and then deliver your response with a completely straight face. Save your amazement and incredulity at these interviewers' questions for when you meet your friends in the pub at the weekend.

Responding To Leading Questions

The commonest pressure questions try to put you on the spot by implying – or perhaps saying outright – something negative about you, leaving you to fight your way uphill to impress the interviewers by countering their insinuations.

To really stand head and shoulders above the other candidates, try to get some of your personality across. Interviewing well isn't just about answering the questions in a technically proficient manner. If you come across as coldly professional and competent, that impression will win you no favours. Try to seem likeable and human – as well as professional and competent, of course.

All of us have personality defects – what is yours?

This is a strongly-worded question and a cunning trap, implying that *everyone* has a personality flaw of some type. Weaker candidates can fall into this trap by exposing some serious failing about themselves. But the cunning response is to deflect the question and actually treat this question as if you have been asked to talk about a minor weakness of yours.

Never talk about any negative characteristics of yourself without also going on to talk about how you compensate for them. So do talk about a minor weakness, but immediately go on to tell the interviewer how you monitor and control that weakness, preventing it becoming an issue at work.

I wouldn't say that I have any personality defects – it's a very strong word. But of course I have areas in which I'm not as strong as others. For example my natural tendency in my personal life is to be quite spontaneous and relaxed about what tasks I need to do and how I run my social life. But I realise that I can't allow myself to become disorganised at work so I always make the effort to spend a few minutes every day thinking about the key tasks I need to achieve and making a list. This allows me to focus on what I need to do and to prioritise how to spend my time.

The candidate here has managed to respond to a potentially leading and very negative question in a positive way.

Why did you not achieve more in your last job?

Another strongly-worded question, this implies that you should apologise for not having become the Chief Executive already. Some candidates may get flustered and start making excuses about what has held them back. Instead, prepare a response to this question that shows what you *are* proud of.

 Talk in a confident manner about the reasons why you are very happy with your career progression so far and either tell the interviewers about what you have learned or reiterate some of your main career achievements:

> ✔ *I'm actually very happy with my career progression so far. Even though I still have the same job title, I have actually learnt a huge amount. When I started the job as an Assistant Buyer two years ago, I had no experience of buying whatso-ever. Whereas now when my manager is away on holiday, she allows me to represent our department at client meet-ings – so I feel that I have gained a lot in skills, experience, and client credibility. I'm now ready for the next step in my career, which is what brings me here today.*

> ✔ *I don't see achievement purely in terms of promotions and rising up the hierarchy. It has always been more important for me to enjoy the job and feel that I am learning new skills. I was asked to apply for a promotion but that would have meant that I'd be managing a team of trainers rather than doing hands-on training, so I turned it down.*

If your CV makes it obvious that you really could have achieved more, then you may need to make that admission. But go on to explain exactly why you have been caught in that rut. I've heard candidates use perfectly respectable reasons such as:

> ✔ An illness in the family – which can include yourself.

> ✔ Long-term disability of a child or family member.

✔ Needing to stay in a geographic area in order to keep a child at school during their GCSEs or A Levels.

✔ Other personal circumstances such as wanting to focus on bringing up a child or having to deal with a tricky divorce.

But go on to explain how those circumstances have changed. Then stress that you are now up for a new challenge and want to kick your career into a higher gear again.

Even though this question is designed to put you on a back foot, be sure to resist the temptation to fabricate a sad story if it isn't true. Remember that employers often check references and are likely to find you out.

How would you respond if I said that you're not the best candidate we've seen today?

An interviewer may ask this question with a hint of a sneer in their tone of voice to see how you cope with disappointment. But you know better than to show any such negative emotion. So instead show your mettle by asking the interviewer: *I'd be very surprised to hear that and I'm very interested to know why you think that. Can you tell me why you think I'm not the best candidate?*

Keep your tone of voice very warm when you ask the interviewer why they think you may not be the best candidate – otherwise, you can risk coming across as abrasive.

Hopefully the interviewer will then give you a couple of reasons that you can counter. For example, if the interviewer says, *I don't think you have enough experience of negotiating deals with suppliers* or *I think you are somewhat lacking in the maturity needed for this role*, then you can tell them your best example of negotiating a deal or a story that illustrates how you dealt with a tricky situation with confidence and maturity.

If the interviewer refuses to give you reasons why they think you are not the strongest candidate they've seen, go on to reiterate some of your key qualities:

Obviously I can't say that I am the very best candidate, as I've not met the other candidates. But what I do know is that I am incredibly determined in my work. I've decided that I want to work in this industry and I'm willing to put in long hours and do whatever it takes to get the job done and build a career in fashion. And my career track record so far should show you that I always achieve what I put my mind to.

How would you rate me as an interviewer?

It *nearly* goes without saying that you should not criticise your interviewer even if you think they *are* disorganised or incompetent. However, neither should you fall into the trap of fawning insincerely and by lavishing too many compliments on the interviewer.

Depending on the style of the interview, choose a response such as:

✔ *I'd say that you are quite a tough interviewer and have asked some very challenging questions that have really forced me to think about how I would deal with different situations. But I would add that being tough on candidates is only fair, as it is a tough job and you want to get an idea of how I would be able to cope with real pressure.*

✔ *I think that you have been a very fair and professional interviewer so far – you have tried to establish a rapport and put me at ease so that I can talk in a relaxed fashion about my skills and experience.*

If you must criticise the interviewer, say that the interview has been very good so far, but that you hope to be given the chance to ask the interviewer some questions about the company and why the interviewer enjoys working there.

What keeps you up at night?

Asking what keeps you up at night is a negative question, implying that you should reveal some deep-seated worries. Describing your worries will almost certainly be taken as a sign of weakness. So your correct answer here is to say that nothing – or almost nothing – keeps you up in a work context.

I can honestly say that nothing keeps me up at night. My job is very important to me, but I always make sure that I do the very best that I can to handle a situation. If a difficult situation or lengthy project needs a lot of work, then I make sure that I make a list at the end of one day so that I can get straight into tackling the most urgent issues the next day. Once I know that I have done the very best that I can, I find that there is nothing to be gained by worrying unduly about something and letting it interfere with my sleep.

If the interviewer continues to pressurise you and says that *something* must keep you up at night, then you may concede by giving an example (briefly) of a work issue that has had you slightly worried in the past.

I sometimes get nervous before big presentations. But when I know that a big presentation is coming up, I take plenty of time to prepare my slides and rehearse my material. I still wouldn't say that a presentation has given me any sleepless nights, but I certainly do wake up in the morning very aware that I need to do some more hard work that day to prepare for it.

Why do you think you are better than the other candidates?

Interviewers asking you this question are trying to lure you into talking about yourself in overly positive and glowing terms.

In most interviews, you won't get to meet the other candidates. Even if you do meet them, you're more likely to exchange nervous smiles and have a polite chat while sitting in reception than to have an in-depth discussion with the other candidates about their skills and experience. So it would be unfathomably arrogant of you to mouth off about why you are better than people that you have no right to comment on.

 Demonstrate an ounce of humility by refusing to compare yourself to people that you can't possibly comment on. Snide comments about other candidates only show you up in a poor light. Instead, stick to talking about your own key qualities.

I don't think I can honestly say that I am better than the other candidates because I have never met them. All I can do is tell you again about my key qualities and why I think I'd be great in this job. I've been told by people that I'm articulate and hard working. I also hope that I've demonstrated my determination and passion for getting into this industry. Hopefully my personality and sense of humour have come across as well. And so all I can do is trust you to make the right decision.

When talking about qualities such as passion, personality, and sense of humour, your facial expression and body language are just as important as conveying a sense of those qualities. Just saying the words with a lifeless face and slumped posture sends out all the wrong signals!

Even if you're applying for an internal post and do know the other candidates, resist the temptation to snipe about them. Pointing out their flaws and weaknesses may reflect badly on you. So stick to your guns and focus on your personal achievement instead.

Responding to Closed Questions

Closed questions such as *Do you take work home with you at weekends?* can technically be answered with just a 'yes' or a 'no'. But you know better than to answer in that way. You also need to explain your reasons why. In fact, it sometimes matters less whether you actually say yes or no than giving a compelling reason why you answered yes or no.

But sometimes neither the 'yes' nor 'no' response is appropriate. On occasion you may need to hedge your bets a little by saying 'it depends', and then go on to explain why you may need to change your behaviour depending on different circumstances.

Do you like regular hours and routine working patterns?

The 'right' answer to this question can very well be a 'yes' or a 'no' depending on the circumstances. For example, if you're applying for work as an ambulance driver, then you are probably going to be working shifts and sometimes crazy hours, meriting one response. But taking on part-time work as part of a job-share may mean that the hours will be very carefully determined weeks in advance.

Look at the job advertisement to get an idea of what the 'right' answer to this question may be. If the description of the job stresses words such as 'flexibility', 'some travel may be expected', 'variety', and 'shift working', then it's likely that the interviewer is looking for you to say that you don't like regular hours and a routine working pattern.

Consider the following two very different responses to the question:

> ✔ *No, because I'd hate to have a job that involved coming into the office at nine o'clock, having an hour's lunch, and then leaving at five thirty every single day. It would bore me rigid, which is exactly why I'm interested in the nature of this job – I like the fact that I could be called upon at short notice to work in different parts of the country and to work either at our branches or a customer's offices. It's the variety that will keep me on my toes.*

> ✔ *Yes. Having a regular working pattern is precisely what I'm looking for. When I saw your advert in the paper looking for someone to work Mondays to Thursdays, I thought that it would suit me perfectly. My daughter has just started at a pre-school group that runs four days a week, so it would give me Fridays off to spend with her. But at the same time, the regularity will give me an opportunity to learn a job and get good at it.*

Do you mind paperwork?

Again, the 'right' answer depends on the nature of the job. But the word 'paperwork' implies bureaucratic shuffling rather than productive work. So even if you do enjoy paperwork, think of another way to put it. For example:

I wouldn't say that I enjoy all paperwork. But I do enjoy being thorough in processing documents. If the contracts aren't signed, then the business could lose a lot of money, so one of the reasons why I'm attracted to this job is that I have a lot of responsibility in ensuring that all of the documentation is correct and up-to-date, and that the right people have access to it in a speedy fashion.

Office-based jobs such as office manager, clerk, personal assistant, or in fact any junior job are likely to involve a fair chunk of paperwork. So prepare your response to the question accordingly.

If applying for a job as a sales person or a consultant, however, you'd expect most of your time to be spent face-to-face with customers or clients. So you may say:

I can't say that I'm the biggest fan of paperwork and I'd much rather be out on the road meeting customers and suppliers. But I realise that it needs doing – otherwise the rest of the team back in the office wouldn't know what orders have been placed. So I make an effort to get all of my paperwork done at the end of the day. With every job goes some elements that are less enjoyable, but it doesn't make them any less important or essential.

If the post is managerial, with people in your team or perhaps a secretary to support you, then it can be acceptable to say that while you personally don't enjoy paperwork, you always ensure that you have competent people around you who can do it.

Have you ever broken the rules to get a job done?

The trap in this question is that a 'yes' answer can label you as a maverick rule breaker, while a categorical 'no' can make you come across as an inflexible worker.

A big difference exists between breaking a rule occasionally to achieve a benefit for your organisation and flagrantly breaking rules because you find them restrictive.

When answering this question, explain that you broke a rule only because you had to react quickly to a situation that would otherwise have meant that your employer would have lost out. Adding that you 'technically' may have broken the rules but that others in the team agreed that it was the right course of action, can be a good idea too.

I have broken the rules, but only because it would otherwise have cost our company thousands of pounds. We were on a deadline to get hundreds of brochures printed and delivered to a customer by Friday afternoon. I'm supposed to get my boss to sign off on spend of over £500, but she fell ill suddenly a few days before the deadline. So I went ahead and ordered the printing and got the brochures delivered to the customer because it was what we had discussed doing any way. When my boss got back, she agreed that it had been the right thing to do. So while I have on occasion technically broken the rules, I only did it because I had the interests of the business in mind.

Do you take work home with you at weekends?

Answering that you don't take work home at weekends can make you appear inflexible; answering that you do take work home can make you sound ineffective during the week. So answer this question by finding a happy medium between the two options.

I rarely find that I need to take work home with me at the weekend. I make a habit of doing as much as I can in the office and I find that it's easier to work when you have your colleagues available to discuss ideas with. Having said that, though, at busy times of the year – for example at year end – I do find myself working all hours to get everything done before the auditors come in.

In answering this question, think about the nature of the industry that you want to work in. If it is commonly known that successful people in this type of job often take work home with them, then you may have to let the interviewer know that you are willing to do so as well.

Do you have any doubts about your ability to do the job?

Employers are looking for confident workers who can get on with the job at hand. I've never seen a job description where they are looking for insecurity as a desirable trait! So even if you are seeking a much bigger promotion and do secretly harbour some doubts, let your response show off your more confident side. Be careful, however, not to sound arrogant by demeaning the job and making it sound as if you think you can do it in your sleep.

If you think that the interviewer has some doubts about your ability, try to second-guess what they may be worried about and go on to reassure them that the job is within your abilities.

I know that this is a significant leap for me to take on managerial responsibility, but I've actually been readying myself for it for about a year now. Even though I have not formally had a team to manage before, I have deputised for my manager on a number of occasions when she has been on holiday or out of the office. So I have actually run the rest of the team of four people for up to a week at a time and delegated to them, checked their work, and made sure that they were happy.

Don't you think you are overqualified for this job?

The interviewer may be worried that the job is too easy for you and that you may quickly get bored of it and want to move on. If you don't think that you are overqualified, then you can ask: *It's interesting that you see me as overqualified. What is it exactly that makes you think that?* You can then counter any objections or worries that the interviewer may have.

But if you think that you actually probably are overqualified, make sure that you have other compelling reasons to explain why you will stick at the job. For example, you can talk about wanting a better work/life balance or wanting to join a smaller company where you have more say in the direction of the business.

Example answers include:

- ✔ *I realise that I've been managing a team of sales people in my last two roles. But what I've come to notice more recently is that I actually enjoy dealing with customers much more than I do managing the team. You could say that I have too much experience, but for me, this is much more about finding a role that I really enjoy rather than doing the one that looks better on my CV and pays more.*

- ✔ *I've spent most of the last three years travelling extensively and the truth is that I miss my family. My children are growing up very quickly and I don't want to miss it. Don't get me wrong as I still really enjoy my job, but I need to find something that will give me a bit more stability.*

Would you have any problems relocating?

Chapter 2 deals with the importance of reading the original job advertisement and other literature when researching and preparing for an interview – so make sure that you don't get caught out by this question.

If relocation was never mentioned, then ask why this question has come up. But never say that you are unwilling to move as it may close the door on the job entirely.

You can then choose from one of the following lines of response:

> ✔ *I understand that I'll be based in this office until the end of the year, but that you are thinking of relocating to amalgamate with some of the other functions down in Basingstoke. That's a big plus when it comes to this job as my partner has just accepted a job in the south-east of England and that's one of the reasons that has prompted me to look for a new job.*

> ✔ *I'm sorry, but I didn't realise that relocation was a possibility. I didn't see any mention of it in the job advert or anything on your Web site. But relocation isn't out of the question as what I've heard so far about this unique role makes it sound ideal for me. Could you tell me a bit more about the proposed relocation please?*

Do you mind travelling?

Just like the last question about relocation, you should already know whether much travel is associated with the job before you step into the interview room.

You can then tailor your response as appropriate:

> ✔ *I get a real buzz out of travel. There are some people who moan about having to travel, but it's not a chore for me as I really enjoy driving/flying/taking trains.*

> ✔ *I don't mind having to travel occasionally with work. For example I had to travel with the Marketing Director a couple of times a year and spent a couple of nights each time in Manchester and Edinburgh. But am I right to think that this job will primarily be based in this office?*

Fending Off Weird and Wonderful Questions

Certain interviewers like to think of themselves as pop psychologists. These people may have read an article once or know someone who knows someone who is a psychologist – and they now believe that certain questions can allow them to peel aside your defences and delve into your personality.

Now, the truth of the matter is that the following questions would never be asked by anyone who has even a half-decent understanding of psychology. But as this is an interview and there are certain rules to abide by, you must simply grit your teeth and smile sweetly in the face of these truly, outstandingly bizarre questions.

Be careful not to sound too rehearsed when responding to the following questions. The idea in a pressure interview is to come across as cool and collected, but not as if you have memorised your answers off by heart. If you answer straightaway without any hesitation at all, then the interviewers may see through you. So make sure that you at least pretend to give each question a moment's thought!

See this pencil I'm holding? Sell it to me

You may expect this question to be asked of people going into sales, but in fact it tends to be asked mainly when interviewers want to put non-sales people under pressure. The interviewers are trying to frighten you with a seemingly odd request.

You can potentially be asked to sell just about anything in sight, from a notebook to the desk at which the interviewers are sitting.

Sales people have to be good mannered, polite, and enthusiastic. Make sure that your tone of voice, facial expressions, and body language display those qualities in answering this question. Passing this question is not just a case of saying the right words – it is just as important for you to appear as if you believe in the words, too.

A good tack may be to follow four simple steps to selling anything:

1. Ask the interviewer some questions to establish his need for the item. For example if you are asked to sell a potted plant: *Do you already own any potted plants? Would you like to own any more?* The interviewer is bound to say no to your questions, which leads onto the next step.

2. Talk about the features and qualities of the item. Describe the shape and texture of the leaves; tell the interviewer about the number of flowers and their colour.

3. Next focus on the benefits of the item. For example, a potted plant may make the room seem greener and more pleasant to work in. It can also relax people who come into the room and make them feel more at home. Plants also generate oxygen and remove stale carbon dioxide.

4. Finally, make a strong statement to finish, such as: *In summary, I think it's a great plant and I'd be delighted to have one of these at home. Would you like one?*

If you follow those steps, your eloquence should suitably impress the interviewer.

Who was your favourite teacher?

Even though the question is asking you to name your favourite teacher, make sure that you are able to explain why he or she was your favourite too. Finish off your answer by reinforcing some quality that you currently possess as a result of your favourite teacher.

A couple of examples:

✔ *Miss Ellwood taught me English until I was 13 years of age. And what has really stayed with me is the way she brought the characters in books to life. She really instilled in me the importance of reading – not just for learning but also for pleasure. So nowadays I make sure that I read a couple of management or business biography books to round out my knowledge.*

✔ *Mr Jackson taught me A Level chemistry. What I liked about his style was that he always made us aware of the fact that what we were learning for our exams was not always the whole truth – that it was a simplified version of what scientists currently understood about chemistry. So it was his teaching style that really filled me with the desire to go on to university to study chemistry and begin a career in science.*

If you were an animal, what would you be?

This question definitely falls into the category of silly pop psychology questions. But remember that you can't tell an interviewer that a question is stupid! The interviewer is wondering how you see yourself. So be sure to pick an animal with suitably positive characteristics.

There's no definitive right answer for choosing what sort of animal you'd be. But lions, tigers, and eagles are generally thought to possess more noble qualities than snakes, weasels, and pigs!

Keep your answer short and sweet in the hope that the interviewer will go on to ask you a more sensible question:

✔ *I'd say I was like a wolf because I'm canny and can smell a good story – which isn't a bad quality in a journalist.*

✔ *I'm like an elephant because I can shoulder a large burden. I can take on lots of work, but also take on the emotional burden of stressed team mates too.*

If you were a cartoon character, who would you be?

Just like the previous question about animals, this is a ridiculous question. But grin and bear it. It almost doesn't matter what character you choose so long as you explain it by talking about some positive, job-related characteristics:

> ✔ *I'm like Hercules in that Disney film. I'm strong and confident – very little gets me down.*

> ✔ *If I had to pick one, I guess I'm like Bugs Bunny. He never gets taken for a ride and always has the last laugh!*

Tell me a story

The pitfall to avoid in answering this question is telling a random story not involving yourself or telling a story that does not sell your career achievements.

The best answer is to talk about your career:

I graduated in 1993 and I've had a variety of roles since then. I started working in a call centre but quickly decided that I wanted a job that allowed me more face-to-face customer contact, so I moved into the hotel industry. I started in a small local chain but got promoted quickly up to desk supervisor and then four years ago to hotel general manager. But I think that I've learned everything that I can from managing that small hotel. And as there have been no opportunities within the company to transfer to another hotel, that's what brings me to this interview today.

Ensure that the interviewer wants to hear this tale by checking first: *Is it okay if I tell you the story of my career?* If the interviewer stops you and insists that you tell the story of your life outside of work, try to squeeze in a couple of facts about your career too:

I was born in Sheffield and grew up there but went to university in Southampton and graduated in 1993. My first job was working in a call centre but then I decided that I wanted to move into a job with more face-to-face contact. In my spare time I'm a keen amateur photographer and a bit of a tennis fanatic. I'm now a general manager managing a hotel with about 120 staff but on the lookout for a bigger hotel to run.

This question is *not* an invitation to tell the interviewer about your entire life in excruciatingly boring detail from the day you were born. Summarise key facts and keep your response under two or three minutes at the very most.

Who do you most admire and why?

Think back to the list of skills that this particular interviewer's organisation is looking for. If they have mentioned financial acumen as a key skill, then talk about a role model who has demonstrated financial acumen. If the employer is on the lookout for tenacity, then pick someone to talk about who has demonstrated determination in his or her life. Some examples:

- ✔ *I really admire Sir Terry Leahy, the Chief Executive of Tesco. He has single-handedly turned around what used to be an ailing supermarket into one of the world's dominant forces in retail. He has engineered the company's expansion into non-food sectors and pushed revenues, profits, and shareholder return up. I aspire to be as good as he is.*

- ✔ *The Sales Director where I used to work was a really great role model. She had two children so always tried to get away by 5.30pm every evening. But she was able to work at such a pace and get such a huge amount done that leaving on time was never an issue. She was incredibly focused and had an amazing ability to prioritise – and I hope that I've picked up some of those traits from her.*

Don't just pick one example of someone you admire for every single interview that you go for. Think through a different answer for every single organisation. Different organisations look for different skills, so your response must reflect that.

If you could meet anyone living or dead, who would it be and why?

Again, as with the question about describing someone that you admire, try to pick someone who has qualities or characteristics that put them (and you) in good stead for the job that you are being interviewed for.

If you have already picked one business leader for your question about who you admire, make sure you have a different leader for this question.

I'd like to meet the first Chief Executive of the National Council for Voluntary Organisations to ask him what made him so passionate about wanting to promote the voluntary organisation sector. Our job of getting people to donate money to charitable causes is becoming increasingly harder work, and I'm sure that he would be an inspirational person to meet.

Be careful of picking politicians unless you are 100 per cent sure of the interviewers' political allegiances. Just as the adage warns you to steer clear of politics and religion at dinner parties, picking a politician from the wrong party can have immediately disastrous consequences for your chances of getting the job!

What is your greatest fear?

Knowing exactly what kind of fear the interviewer is trying to get at is difficult. Ask a question to check before you jump in with the wrong sort of response: *Do you mean a professional fear or a personal fear?* If the interviewer leaves the choice up to you, then talk about a professional fear.

This is quite a negative question. Try to turn the question to your advantage. End your response on a high note by talking up some positive quality about yourself.

Some example responses:

> ✔ *I wouldn't say that I have any fears as such – it's a very strong term. But I do worry occasionally and take very seriously the threat that Internet-based retailers pose for our industry. To me, that means that I must make even greater efforts to make sure that the customers visiting our shops can get a positive customer experience that will keep them coming back to us rather than buying from the Internet.*

> ✔ *Personally, I worry for the future of my children. Growing up nowadays seems to be filled with so many more perils than when we were growing up 30 years ago. But I do the best that I can – I try to instill good values in my children and make sure that they eat well, and I play with them and get them to exercise. It's all a good parent can do.*

Saying Something Is Better Than Saying Nothing

No matter how much preparation you do, you're never going to be able to predict and prepare for every single question that you can come across. And eventually you may get asked a question that you just don't have an answer for. Yes, even I, the great and powerful Dr Yeung, have occasionally been stumped by a question.

Now, you may be tempted to apologise and say, *I don't know.* But you may as well just say, *I'm stupid and I can't think of an answer. I'm a rubbish candidate. Throw my CV into the bin now!*

Playing for time

If you can't think of an answer within the first few seconds, then your first tactic may be to play for time to allow you to think about the question a bit more. But don't just sit there saying nothing.

Silence during an interview can be either perfectly acceptable or excruciatingly painful. If you tell the interviewers that you need a few moments to think about the question, they'll give you a bit of space – but if you don't, they'll start to worry for you – and that is never a good impression to leave them with.

If you don't understand the question, you can perhaps ask for more clarification. Try one of the following:

- ✔ *That's a tough one. I'll need to think about it for a moment.*

- ✔ *That's a really good question. I'm sure there's a really good answer to it, but I'm afraid that you've got me there. Could we perhaps move on and maybe come back to it in a bit?*

- ✔ *You'll have to excuse me but I'm not entirely sure I under- stand the question. Could you rephrase it for me please?*

- ✔ *I'm not familiar with that particular term. Could you just explain that to me please?*

Making a last ditch effort

If you really can't think of how to answer a question, you may be forced to admit it. But if at all possible, try talking up some positive quality about yourself or give a related example to illustrate your skill in a similar area:

✔ *I have to admit that I've never had to deal with that area of responsibility in my current role. However, I'd be very keen to take it on as a responsibility and in fact that's one of the reasons why I'm so excited about the possibility of working for you.*

✔ *I'm sorry but I haven't used that particular software package before. However, I do learn incredibly quickly. For instance, last year I had never used the XYZ package but effectively taught myself how to use it from scratch in about four weeks.*

✔ *I've never been in that precise situation myself with a customer. But something similar did once happen with a colleague. For example. . . .*

Even more bizarre questions

Some interviewers pride themselves on devising fiendish new questions to goad candidates with. Some more genuine questions that I've heard interviewers ask candidates include:

✔ What five famous people would you invite to a dinner party and why?

✔ Why are manhole covers round?

✔ Define true happiness.

✔ Would you rather be famous or powerful?

✔ Do you think the government should increase the national minimum wage or not?

Have a go at answering these questions. The reason the interviewer is asking these questions is to catch you off guard. Even if you don't know the answer, you still have to come up with something convincing. So how would you respond to these off-beat questions?

Chapter 9

Succeeding at Competency-Based Interviewing

*C*ompetency-based interviewing is simply a technique that interviewers use to scrutinise your previous experience to find out whether you have the relevant skills they really need for the job.

Psychologists have discovered that one of the best predictors of whether job candidates will be successful in a job is the past experience they have. Just think about the situation for a moment: If you were looking for a negotiator, wouldn't you rather employ someone who had experience of negotiating deals than someone who can only talk about how she *would* or *may* negotiate? Or if you were looking for a data analyst, wouldn't you feel more confident hiring someone who can talk you through analytical problems he had dealt with in the past than someone who says that he could probably pick it up?

Competencies are just management-speak for 'the skills and behaviours that determine success at work'. So the interviewers look for you to describe the skills you used and how you actually behaved in different work situations.

Discovering the Rules of the Game

The key to excelling at competency-based questions is to always respond by talking about a specific incident in the past that you dealt with. Don't answer by talking about how you *would* handle a situation. And don't talk about how you *generally* handled those kinds of situations in the past.

Talk about a single incident that happened to you. Be ready to relate specific details and even names of other people who were involved, approximate dates, and the locations if necessary.

Also, be ready to talk about your example in a lot of detail. The interviewers will likely bombard you with dozens of questions to find out what the situation was, who was involved, what you did and why you did it, how other people reacted, what you said or did next, how other people changed their reactions, and so on.

A lot of candidates exaggerate their experience to some degree. But the whole point of competency-based interviewing is to catch out liars. Just as the police question suspected criminals, the interviewers fire multiple questions at you in quick succession to get at the truth. You are much more likely to trip yourself up by lying.

Spotting competency-based questions

Competency-based questions often do not sound like questions at all. While most interview questions start with questioning words such as *what*, *when*, *how*, and *why*, competency-based questions tend to sound more like requests.

You can spot competency-based questions because the interviewers instruct you to tell them about particular situations or to give specific examples. Look out for language such as:

- *Give me an example of a time when you. . .*

- *Tell me about an occasion when you. . .*

- *Talk me through a situation that you have been in when. . .*

- *Can you tell me about an instance in which you. . .*

If you hear language like this, the interviewer is almost certain to want a specific example that you have experienced.

Dealing with skilled competency-based interviewers

If an interviewer asks you an initial question and then continues to ask perhaps three or four further questions, you know that you are in safe hands because this is the sign of a very competent and well-skilled interviewer. The sidebar 'Competency-based interviewing at its best' shows an example of the sort of interview you should hope to find yourself in. The interviewer is likely to have been trained in the skills of competency-based interviewing – in other words, how to dig the information out of you. Simply follow the interviewer's lead and describe how you handled that specific situation.

Be sure to read the following section, 'Dealing with unskilled competency-based interviewers' in case you find yourself dealing with an interviewer who isn't skilled in this technique.

Always talk about what you did in the first person singular by saying *I did*, *I spoke*, *I suggested*, and so on. Avoid describing what *we* did too much. After all, whom are you trying to get a new job for – you or your entire team?

Competency-based interviewing at its best

Here's a worked example of a good competency-based interviewer speaking to a candidate. As you can see, a skilled interviewer asks as many questions as necessary to establish exactly what happened and how you resolved a situation.

Interviewer: *Tell me about the last time you faced a problem and how you tackled it.*

Candidate: *This was about two months ago. As I mentioned earlier, I work in a team of five accountants reporting to the accounts manager. We discovered that a computer virus had corrupted most of the reports that we had to hand in at the end of the month. And so we had about three days to do over a week's worth of work.*

Interviewer: *Going back to the beginning, how did you first discover the virus problem?*

Candidate: *It wasn't me who discovered it. Our accounts clerk found the problem and shouted it around the room. She was panicking and getting really stressed out. And the first thing I did when I saw this was to sit her down and get her to tell the rest of us exactly what the problem was.*

Interviewer: *So what happened next?*

Candidate: *I suggested that we check whether we had viable back-ups but unfortunately the virus had infiltrated our system before the weekly back-up had been done.*

Interviewer: *So what did you do next?*

Candidate: *We brainstormed ideas and decided to get help from the finance department of another business unit. Doing so wasn't standard practice, but I suggested the idea to my boss, who agreed it was the right thing to do. And so we ended up getting all of the accounts completed by the end of the month.*

Interviewer: *Sorry, can I go back in time a little bit. You said 'we'. What was your role in that brainstorming process?*

Candidate: *I say 'we', but it was my suggestion to initiate a brainstorm. I laid down some rules for the brainstorm – that we would come up with as many ideas as possible before critiquing them.*

Interviewer: *What other options did you come up with and how did you decide to get help from the other finance department?*

Candidate: *The main other option was to hire temporary staff to help us with processing the data. But that would have cost over £1000. Someone else in the team then joked that it was a shame we couldn't get the accounts team based at our other office to help us and I thought it was a good idea. No one had done it before, but I thought it may be worth giving a go, so I said that I would sug-*

gest the proposed solution to my boss.

Interviewer: *And how did your boss respond to the idea?*

Candidate: *He didn't like the suggestion initially. But I showed him the cost analysis of how expensive it* would be to get temporary staff in. And I said that I had already checked that our other office wasn't busy. So eventually he let me bring their team to our office for a few days.

Interviewer: *Thank you. Let's move on to the next question now. . . .*

Dealing with unskilled competency-based interviewers

Although many interviewers are skilled at asking competency-based questions, many other interviewers merely dabble in the technique. They ask an initial question but then fail to ask any supplementary questions or only ask one or two follow-up questions. The danger is that if you don't tell the interviewers what they need to know, they may score you down for not possessing the right skills. So the challenge in this situation is for you to answer the questions that they should be – but aren't – asking.

You can spot unskilled interviewers by counting the number of follow-up questions that they ask. If interviewers ask less than two further questions, then you may need to give more lengthy responses than you had to with skilled competency-based interviewers, (see the sidebar 'Competency-based interviewing at its worst').

If you're not satisfied that the interviewer knows enough about the skills that you used in a particular situation, you may even need to politely interrupt him and provide him with an additional few sentences to describe exactly what you did in a given situation.

Competency-based interviewing at its worst

Just as some interviewers are great at asking competency-based questions, others are less skilled. If you find yourself in this situation, follow the lead of the candidate in the following example to help you get your point across.

Interviewer: *Tell me about the last time you helped out a colleague.*

Candidate: *This happened a couple of weeks ago. I noticed that one of my colleagues, John, was just sitting there with his head in his hands. He was just staring at his computer screen but not actually doing any work. So I thought I'd help him out.*

Interviewer: *Thank you. Moving on to the next question. . . .*

Candidate: *Actually, can I just add something to that last question about my colleague? I hadn't initially realised what the problem was, so I took him to the canteen and sat him down. He was really down but eventually with a bit of listening, I found out that he'd just heard that he'd lost his biggest customer to a competitor. So he was really worried that he was going to be fired. To cut the rest of the story short, I suggested that he warn our boss that he was going to miss his target for the month. And then I worked with him to create an action plan to find a new customer, which we managed to do over the course of a few months.*

In this example, the candidate gives additional information to demonstrate a number of further skills. First, that the candidate possessed empathy and sensitivity. Second, that the candidate was able to make useful suggestions. Third, that the candidate was able to support a colleague in creating an action plan.

Identifying Likely Questions

You may be a bit disheartened by the need to prepare for so many different competency-based questions. In an actual interview, however, some of the questions covered in this chapter may simply never apply to you. The type of questions asked depend on the sort of job that you're going for. And, in practice, you can actually anticipate many of the questions that the interviewers are likely to ask you.

Take a look at the original job advert for the interview you're attending (refer to Chapter 2 for more on this) and try to pull out the main skills and qualities that the interviewers are looking for.

Consider the excerpt from a job advert, shown in Figure 9-1, where I've underlined the job's main skills and qualities. From this advert, expect to have questions about all the underlined skills, such as:

☛ *Tell us about a time that you dealt with a difficult customer.*

☛ *Give us an example of a time when you negotiated something with a customer or colleague.*

☛ *Can you give us an example of an occasion when you have been knocked back, but then had to motivate yourself again?*

☛ *Tell us about an instance when you had to be flexible at work.*

☛ *Can you tell me about an occasion when you had to organise a project?*

XYZ Company

We're looking for people to join our team as Client Liaison Officers (CLOs). CLO candidates must have excellent <u>customer service skills</u>, as you will be dealing with customers face-to-face and on the telephone on a daily basis. You must also have good <u>negotiation skills</u>. In addition, you should be <u>self-motivated</u>, <u>flexible</u>, and able to <u>organise your own workload</u>.

Figure 9-1: Highlighting the key skills in a job advert.

Or consider the excerpt from a job advert shown in Figure 9-2. Again, the four key competencies are underlined. So be sure to prepare for questions such as:

☛ *Tell us about a team that you have led.*

☛ *Talk me through how you have coached or developed a member of your team.*

> ✔ *Can you talk me through a time that you had to think strategically in terms of running your team?*
>
> ✔ *Tell me about a time when you improved the profitability of your team or division.*

We want you!

JKL International seeks a new regional manager to <u>lead a team</u> of more than 100 staff spread across three branches. You must be excited by <u>coaching and developing</u> your team and see yourself as a manager with the ability to <u>think strategically</u> and <u>improve the profitability</u> of the region.

Figure 9-2: More qualities to pick out in a job advert.

 Always talk about specific examples. Be ready to explain a situation, the task you were faced with, the actions you took, and the result that you achieved.

Questions about Your Thinking and Planning Skills

Interviewers often break down competencies into different categories. And interviewers often put great emphasis on recruiting employees with judgement and decision-making, organizing, and planning skills.

 You're okay to take a few moments to think of an example to competency-based questions. If you haven't prepared a good example beforehand, just say: *That's a tough question, can I think about it for a few moments?* Don't panic!

Tell me about a significant project that you managed

When asked about a significant project that you've managed, be aware that the interviewers are not only interested in what the project was, but also in how you organised it and made it happen. In answering this question, make sure that you tell the interviewers how you planned the project and then subsequently delivered it.

Have a personal example to talk about. Be ready to talk about when you managed a project, what the project was, why you were given the piece of work initially, and what actions you took in order to make it a success.

A junior candidate may talk about a less significant project, such as:

I was asked to organise the Christmas party for our 25 staff and given a budget of £50 per head. I started by sending out an e-mail to everyone in the office to check whether they preferred to have the party on a Friday night after work or on a Saturday, and the majority favoured Saturday. I then rang up nearby hotels to find out costs. Most were quite expensive but I found three or four that were within our budget. I asked them to fax over menus and I looked on their Web sites to check the quality of the hotels. I eventually found two hotels that fit our criteria so I went to visit them both. I thought that one seemed a grander venue so negotiated a deal with them. Then nearer the time, I sent out invitations and handled people's requests for vegetarian options. The party was a big success and my boss was really pleased.

Now give me an example of a project that went wrong

In an interview, be ready to talk about projects that didn't turn out so well, along with those that did. Whenever you tell an interviewer about a situation that you handled well – such as in answering 'Tell me about a significant project that you managed' (see the preceding section) – you may also get asked about a situation that didn't work out so well.

Consider this answer:

About three months ago, our sales director asked me to arrange a breakfast meeting for a dozen clients served by our Manchester office. I began by checking with our sales team when would be a good date to run the breakfast meeting and we chose a date in 8 weeks' time. I then looked up on our system to find out our largest clients. Then I rang up our clients to invite them to the breakfast meeting. I also wrote out a script so that I could get across the key points of why they should turn up to the meeting. Doing so took me around three days, but ultimately I got 15 clients to sign up. I figured that even with a few cancellations, we would still end up with 12 people turning up on the day itself. The organisation of the event went swimmingly until the day itself. That was the day back in January when we had all that snow, so 12 clients cancelled and only three turned up. Of course, the event was a waste of money, but there was nothing that any of us could have done differently.

 Talking about failure is okay as long as you can show that you did everything in your power to attempt to deal with a situation, but that it failed because of circumstances out of your control.

 Make sure that you can explain any lessons that you learned from a project or piece of work that went wrong.

Give me an example of a difficult decision that you have made

Be ready to talk about a difficult decision you've had to make and why it was difficult. For example, was the decision tough because you had to deal with many sources of information and the right choice was unclear? Or was the decision tricky because of the emotional impact or consequences on yourself or other people? This example demonstrates what I mean:

I was asked by my manager at head office to review options for cutting costs in my office by £85,000 per year. I knew that it was going to be a painful process and I didn't want my staff to worry unduly so I took my three supervisors and our finance manager for an away-day session on a Saturday afternoon. We decided that we could trim some costs – such as payment of overtime, training budgets, and staff entertainment – by a bit. But I realised that we really needed to make a handful of redundancies to meet the target. I asked my finance manager to do a cost-benefit analysis of which staff would need to go. The following week, when she came back with her recommendations, I sent a copy to my area manager. Once my manager approved the finance manager's recommendations, I discussed the final decision with my supervisors. And then I asked for those four employees to come into my office one at a time so I could tell them face-to-face. Of course, these employees were upset, but I assured them that the decision wasn't personal and that we would give them good references. Making these people redundant was one of the toughest decisions I've ever had to make, but it was the only option given what our head office was asking us to do.

Interviewers are much more interested in work decisions than personal ones. Avoid talking about personal decisions such as whether to move house, start a family, or get divorced.

Interviewers like to hear about any analytical techniques you used or even just brainstorming ideas weighing up pros and cons.

Talk to me about a mistake you made and what you did to rectify it

When asked about a mistake, pick a work-related mistake you made, and then focus your attention on describing the actions you took to resolve the situation. For example:

I've been part of the team manning the IT helpdesk for six months now and this incident happened about a month after I started. One of the team was on maternity leave and another was off sick, so I allowed a junior trainee to fill in for two shifts a week. Unfortunately, a couple of people in the company rang me up to complain that they had been given bad advice that had made their computers freeze up. So, of course, I had to apologise profusely to these colleagues and sort out their problem. Then I had to take the trainee aside and explain the error he'd made. I made sure to explain that the mistake wasn't his fault as it had been my decision to put someone unqualified on the helpdesk. Making sure the trainee understood the correct way of handling that problem was more important than shouting at him.

Saying that you have never made a mistake makes you appear defensive. Don't fall into this trap.

Questions about Leading and Managing

If applying for a job that involves managing or supervising any employees, you're likely to be asked about your experiences of being in charge of others.

At one time, managers used to use a style of management known as *command and control* – bossing the team around, checking up on them, and punishing them when they didn't get the work done properly. However, most modern organisations are looking for more empowering managers who can motivate and support rather than bark orders and chastise.

Tell me about a time you inspired a team

You may think that you have never 'inspired' anyone. But try to think of an occasion when you motivated or encouraged others – even if it was just one person.

Check out this for an answer:

The management team had decided to restructure the business for the second time in 18 months and everyone was feeling negative about the prospect of yet more upheaval. I decided that we needed to inject some spirit into the team, so I set up a competition. We took a Friday afternoon off from our normal work and I told everyone that I would be splitting them into three teams to compete in coming up with novel ideas for servicing our customers in the wake of the restructure. Whichever team devised the best ideas for how to improve our performance would win a case of wine. They came up with some really good ideas and we had a lot of fun. Afterwards, the team was a lot more energised than they would have been if I hadn't initiated the team competition event.

 You can talk about inspiring others in the light of bad news such as a restructuring or redundancies. Or you can talk about inspiring people after receiving good news, such as a business opportunity that you motivated your team to strive for.

Talk me through how you coached or developed a team member

Employers want to hire people who can help others to improve their skills. Make sure that you can share an example that shows the interviewers how you took time to understand a member of your team's weaknesses and then set about tackling those weaknesses together.

Here's a good example:

When I joined my current company, I was asked to manage an existing team of sales people. One of them wasn't hitting his sales targets and my manager said that we may need to let him go. I decided to give him a last chance, so sat him down and we talked about his performance. He said that he was fine in making presentations to clients, but wasn't very good at negotiating deals with them – and that's why he wasn't hitting his targets. I offered to help and did a couple of customer roleplays with him so that I could evaluate what he was doing. Next, I gave him advice on what he could be doing better. Once I thought he had the hang of useful techniques, I shadowed him on a couple of customer negotiations. I'm pleased to say that this person really improved and two months later reached his sales targets.

 Coaching typically involves face-to-face discussions, but can also include tools such as shadowing and sending people on training courses.

Tell me about an occasion when you had to deal with a difficult team member

If you possibly can, aim to talk about an occasion when you dealt with a difficult member of the team and turned them around – perhaps through coaching and development – into a productive member of the team.

This example explains a tricky situation in a positive way:

I noticed a few months ago that a bit of conflict existed in our team of technicians in the lab. I talked to each of them individually and the opinion seemed to be that one of them, Mel, was shirking some of her workload. I took Mel out for lunch and asked if everything was okay. She said that everything was fine, so I then had to tell her that I thought the team were experiencing some problems. She got angry and told me to leave her alone, so I did. But after a couple of weeks, I received a complaint about her work again. So I took her aside for a second time and we discussed the problem. She still did not recognise that a problem existed, so I told her that I would allocate work to her on a daily basis. She wasn't happy with my suggestion at first but eventually she came to accept it and the problem appears to have gone away.

 If the interviewers have already asked you for an example of someone that you have coached, talk about someone you had to have hard words with or even discipline.

Questions about Your People and Customer Skills

Even if you're not applying for a job as a manager of any sort, you still need to demonstrate your skills in handling other people. Employers need to know that handling situations ranging from influencing, persuading, and selling, to dealing with difficult colleagues and customers isn't a problem for you.

When talking about how you dealt with another person, remember to mention the full range of communication methods you used from face-to-face meetings through to telephone conversations, e-mail, and even faxes and letters.

Tell me about a time that you persuaded someone to change their mind

Explain to the interviewers a situation when a person – such as a colleague, a customer, your boss, or perhaps a supplier – initially disagreed with your point of view. Then tell them exactly what you said or did to bring the other person round to your viewpoint.

Our department was badly understaffed and a couple of us in the team tried to persuade our editor that we needed to take on a junior staff writer. Jackie, the editor, was against the idea because she said that we didn't have the budget. I knew that she would never listen to a member of her team, so I mentioned the idea to one of the other editors and persuaded this other editor to talk to Jackie. The other editor managed to persuade Jackie because Jackie tends to respect her peers more than her team.

Another common variant on this question is for interviewers to ask: *Can you give me an example of a time that you had to adapt your communication style to meet someone else's needs?* Your response would still follow the approach taken in this example.

Talk to me about a difficult colleague you've worked with

Talk about how you turned an initially bad relationship into a more amicable one. Organisations want employees who can use their communication skills to foster effective working relationships – by asking tactful questions, listening, demonstrating empathy, and being assertive when necessary.

Here's an example of a suitable answer:

Four other administrators work in our office and the most senior of them has always had a bit of a temper. Even trivial matters annoy him and he tends to blame others for his own mistakes. I've tried to have a decent discussion with him about his work or projects that have gone wrong, but he refuses to accept responsibility. His attitude was beginning to affect the quality of our work, so eventually I decided to talk to our manager. I explained to the manager that I didn't want to get this administrator into trouble, but that his behaviour was affecting our work. My manager had a few words with him, and this other administrator has been a lot better since then.

If you can't honestly talk about having turned a relationship around, then make sure that you can at least demonstrate how you managed to work effectively with a difficult colleague.

Have you ever had to give someone negative feedback at work? How did it go?

This question is very similar to *Talk to me about a difficult colleague you've worked with* (dealt with in the preceding section). However, in answering this question, you must demonstrate that you gave the colleague a piece of advice that changed their subsequent behaviour.

This response does just that:

We work in an open plan office and focusing on your work when other people are talking loudly on the phone or to each other can be quite difficult. One of my colleagues has a loud voice and tends to laugh quite loudly too. He also bellows on the phone and given that his job is to call clients, it was really getting on the nerves of the rest of the team. So one day I took him out for a coffee and said really politely that he had a very loud voice and that it was annoying quite a few of us. He was really mortified and said he didn't realise he was being such a nuisance. Since then he has made a huge effort to keep his voice down.

 A good management adage is to 'praise publicly, criticise privately'. So the best time to give negative feedback is always in a one-to-one discussion rather than an open confrontation.

Tell me about a time you used your personal network to business advantage

Interviewers are most likely to ask this question when the job involves selling or business development. But networking is also a useful skill in many jobs for keeping tabs on what competitors are up to and finding out what customers want.

Here's an example showing how you've networked successfully:

My job is to set up service contracts with corporate clients and it helps to have a good network. I used my personal network last week, actually – I was putting together a proposal for one client and did not know how low I should price our offering in order to win the bid. Luckily, the operations director of the organisation seeking the quote used to work at another company with whom I've done business, so I gave him a ring. He hinted that the purchasing director was more interested in the quality of service than price. So I really focused on quality in our presentation and as a result we've been short listed for the next round of bidding.

Tell me about a time you sold something to a customer

Interviewers usually ask this question of candidates applying for sales jobs. If you have never sold a product or service to an external customer, then talk about when you sold an idea to an internal customer (a colleague).

Remember that a 'sale' doesn't necessarily need to be anything too grand:

When I was at university, I had a part-time job in a women's clothing shop. I remember one time when a woman came in wanting a summer dress for a wedding reception she was going to. She tried on several dresses but didn't like any of them. I chatted to her about the wedding and asked what other people would be wearing. She said that everyone else would probably be wearing summer dresses so I suggested to her that she buck the trend by buying a blouse and skirt combination. She loved the idea and spent over £200 on a complete outfit.

Effective selling is not only about *pushing* products on customers by telling them about features and benefits. Effective selling is also about top salespeople talking about the need for *pulling* customers into buying the product by asking questions and establishing what customers like and need.

Give me an example of a time you exceeded a customer's expectations

Organisations assume that you can meet a customer's expectations in terms of being polite and delivering what they expect. But what they really want is candidates who exceed expectations and delight customers. In fact, a lot of organisations use the slightly cheesy term *customer delight* to describe what they're hoping to achieve.

This example demonstrates great customer service:

We had a really big printing job on recently. The customer had asked for the materials to be ready for them to pick up on Friday afternoon, but they rang to say that they were running late. Unfortunately, our shop was due to close at 5 p.m. and the customer was worried about getting to us on time. I suggested arranging a courier to deliver the materials and the customer thought it was a great idea. But because it was such a big job, I knew that the cost of a courier was relatively small – so I said that I'd also send the courier free of charge. The customer was absolutely over the moon and has been using us ever since.

If you can, tell the interviewers that you took the initiative to do something out of the ordinary.

 Do tell the interviewers if you received a letter of thanks from a customer, praise from your manager, or repeat business as a result of your initiative.

Questions about Your Personal Effectiveness

One key group of competencies focuses on employees' ability to motivate and develop themselves. When you face setbacks, you need to be able to get up and get on with the job. And when you spot a weakness – perhaps an area of skill, knowledge, or even a personality trait – in yourself, you need to be able to work on that weakness and better yourself. The questions in this section are geared toward helping you prepare answers for personal questions.

Tell me about a time that you failed to achieve your goals

Don't say that you have never failed to achieve your goals because it just sounds unbelievable. Your best bet is to describe a situation when you did not achieve everything that you set out to do – a partial failure rather than a complete failure:

Every month I assemble a report for our area manager. I have to get information from four departments and write an introduction and executive summary for the whole report. Two months ago, I e-mailed each of the department heads and asked them to write the couple of pages that I needed and told them when I would need the information. Three departments gave me the information on time, but one did not. I chased him by e-mail and phone, but he didn't respond. So I went to this department head's office in person, but he said that he had been too busy and that the earliest he could get the information together would be two days after my deadline for the report. However, I persuaded him to spend just ten minutes with me telling me most of what I needed to know so that I could write his section of the report. I managed to cobble something together, but everyone knew that that section of the report was not as strong. I did everything that I could, but I'm afraid that I didn't produce as good a report as I normally do.

With negatively phrased questions such as this, try to illustrate how you did everything possible, but failed because of circumstances out of your control.

A common variation on this question is: *Talk to me about an occasion you failed to meet a deadline*. Again, the best strategy is to talk about just missing a deadline because of extremely unusual circumstances.

How did you respond to the last piece of criticism you received?

Candidates who say that they don't listen to constructive criticism may as well say that they're going to be difficult to manage – can you imagine having someone working for you who won't listen to your constructive criticism? This question is related to 'How do you take personal criticism?' (see Chapter 5).

Try working out a response similar to this example:

Perhaps three or four months ago, my boss said that I didn't always have very good listening skills. I think that I always do listen when I'm in meetings, so I was a bit taken aback. I asked her what she meant and after a bit of thought she said that on occasion she'd seen me not looking at the person speaking or even engaging in doodling on my notepad. I accepted the feedback – I do have a tendency to doodle when I'm bored. And even when I'm actually listening, I don't always look at the person who's talking. But I've taken both bits of criticism on board and make an effort to not only listen, but to look as if I'm listening too.

If you don't accept feedback automatically, you need to say so and then be sure to explain that you challenge and ask questions to make sure that the feedback is justified.

Give me an example of how you have developed yourself

When outlining ways that you've developed yourself, make sure to indicate that you were aware of a development need and then took steps to meet that need. For example, simply talking about courses that your manager insisted you go on doesn't show your own personal enthusiasm for professional development!

Mention a development need that arose in your last appraisal. Alternatively, think about the skill areas where you used to be – but are no longer – weak.

Here are two examples of ways in which you, as a candidate, can say that you've developed yourself:

> ✔ *In my last performance evaluation, my manager suggested that I needed to become more familiar with the basics of employment law to add more value to the line managers that I support. So I researched appropriate courses and how much they cost. I made a proposal to my manager and he signed off for me to attend a two-day workshop on the topic back in November. Since then, I've become much more comfortable discussing with line managers the rules and potential problems associated with hiring and firing decisions.*

> ✔ *I've worked quite hard on developing my sales skills. I've always had good customer skills, but until recently had never had to sell to customers. When I first started working in my current job, I didn't really understand that we would have sales targets to reach and I struggled to achieve them. So I watched some of the good sales assistants and tried to pick up on some of the techniques and phrases they used. Over the last year or so, I have been working hard at improving my sales skills and I've been meeting my targets for the last three months.*

Don't forget to talk in the first person when describing what happened. Use phrases such as *I did . . .* or *I decided to . . .* rather than *My manager told me to . . .*

Part III
Dealing with Tricky Questions and Other Situations

"Just what _is_ the reason you're leaving your present employer, Mr Flembottle?"

In this part . . .

*I*nterviewers can be a fiendish and dastardly lot. They set out to discover your weak spots and deliberately ask questions that will make you squirm. Perhaps your weak spot is a period of unemployment, a change of direction in your career, or simply even your age (older or younger than the other candidates). You may be dreading questions about your health, too. Or maybe your weak spot is your aptitude with numbers or being able to handle questions about tricky hypothetical situations. Some interviewers even ask questions that can make you feel uncomfortable because they are unnecessarily intrusive – or even illegal. In this part, I show you how to deal with these sorts of difficult questions.

Chapter 10

Responding to Questions for Graduates and School Leavers

. . . .

In This Chapter

▶ Showing off your higher education experience in the best possible light

▶ Talking convincingly about your time at school

. . . .

A lot of interviewers say that they would rather interview candidates who have a few years of work experience rather than graduates or school leavers. Interviewers often say that graduates and school leavers don't have anything interesting to talk about. So your job is to prove those interviewers wrong (with a bit of help from this chapter).

Questions for Graduates

Interviewers want to hire graduates who have some direction and purpose in their lives. The truth is that quite a lot of young people (me included!) went to university mainly because their parents or school expected them to, rather than because they carefully weighed up the opportunities and options available to them. However, telling that to an interviewer is career suicide.

Many of the questions in this section are relevant if you've recently completed any sort of course or professional qualification – from an MBA to an NVQ. So for 'university', the interviewers can equally substitute 'college', 'business school', 'academy', or the name of your training body or organisation.

With all the following questions, the interviewers are looking for evidence that you weighed up pros and cons and came to a sensible choice.

If you're reading this chapter after dropping out of university, without actually graduating, see the sidebar 'Why did you leave before you had finished your course?' for help with your answer.

Why did you choose to go to the university you went to?

The candidates who give the best answers to this question are likely to mention that they did careful and thorough research on the reputation of the particular department and the subsequent employability of graduates leaving that course. A lot of graduates also talk about the importance of having good facilities and physical resources such as libraries and laboratories.

Saying that you were attracted to a particular city or location because of its lively social life is okay. But mention this only after you have listed three or four other, more compelling reasons.

Having done biology, history, and maths at school, I knew that I wanted to read psychology so I researched the top departments in the country. However, I decided that I wanted a four-year course that offered an industry placement, as I felt that having a year's practical work experience would put me in a much stronger position than graduates who had spent three years studying theory without experiencing its application.

Many people accept places at university through the clearing system. If this applies to you, still explain why you decided to take the offer you were made.

I was offered my place through clearing. My priority in deciding whether to take it or not was to ensure that I would still be picking up useful skills that would make me employable in business.

When I rang the department to ask more about the course, they talked about the kinds of jobs that graduates end up in. And certainly, you've invited me for an interview today – and this is my dream job – so it was the right choice at the time to accept the offer.

Your university results aren't very good – why is that?

If you honestly have a good reason why you were not able to perform to the best of your ability – such as personal illness or extremely difficult family circumstances – then of course mention it.

If you do not have a compelling reason, try to convince the interviewers that you are simply more suited to the world of work than studying.

Why did you leave before you had finished your university course?

Quitting before you graduate can be quite a blot on your CV. Make sure that you have a compelling reason why you decided to leave.

If you can, try to talk about the options that you considered before quitting.

✔ *I thought the course would be a good way to pursue a career in the music industry. But after the first year, I realised that I wasn't learning anything I hadn't already learned in some of my part-time jobs and work experience. I spent quite a long time thinking about it – leaving my course wasn't a snap decision. But ultimately*

I decided to leave rather than waste another two years and thousands of pounds going over skills that I've already acquired.

✔ *I started the course because I've always wanted to work in finance. But I quickly discovered that I wasn't ready to spend three years doing a degree. I wanted to enter the workforce and earn a living for a while. I'm still keen to pursue further qualifications, but intend to do a practical part-time course while I continue to work rather than do a theoretical full-time course.*

Even though I only got a lower second overall, you'll see that I actually got an upper second for my assessed essays and final-year dissertation. I have to admit that I've always found written exams very difficult because I find it hard to memorise large volumes of information. But I excel in practical work when a project is more open-ended and I can use my resourcefulness. And I believe that the kind of work I would be doing in your company would be based more on research and analytical skills than learning facts off by heart.

Why did you choose your degree subject?

The interviewer is interested in whether you made an informed decision or not. Mention any research you did and how you weighed up pros and cons.

Take a look at these examples:

- *I enjoyed maths at A Level, but didn't want to plump for a subject purely because I enjoyed it. So I got some prospectuses from mathematics departments and did some research on the Web. When I found out that maths graduates go on to all sorts of careers – 85 per cent of graduates go into careers unrelated to mathematics – I decided that it wouldn't curtail my later career options.*

- *I went to a couple of university open days and visited the politics departments and learnt quite a bit about the nature of the subject. What most influenced me was the fact that a degree in politics gives you the skills to analyse and deconstruct arguments, which I thought would be invaluable in whatever profession I ended up in.*

What have you learnt from being at university?

Interviewers are rarely interested in the exact content of your degree unless you studied a vocational course such as medicine or engineering and are applying for jobs in that field. If you think such questions may apply to you, check out the sidebar 'Answering technical questions about your course'. Instead, think about the skills that you picked up, such as:

- ✔ Researching; gathering qualitative or quantitative data; analysing data; critically evaluating arguments.

- ✔ Writing reports and presenting information at tutorials or seminars.

- ✔ *Multi-tasking* – Juggling multiple assignments or part-time work or other commitments outside of studying.

- ✔ Working in teams with other students.

- ✔ Raising funds, managing budgets, and organising events on behalf of societies or charities.

Answering technical questions about your course

Most degrees in the UK are *non-vocational* – they rarely prepare you for any specific career. For example, a chemistry graduate can easily retrain to become a lawyer or primary school teacher. Or a psychology graduate may decide to go into management consultancy or accountancy. As such, interviewers are usually more interested in your transferable skills and less interested in the exact nature of your course.

However, you can never tell what an interviewer may ask! A minority of interviewers may want to hear about some of the more detailed aspects of your course. Be ready to answer more factual questions such as:

- ✔ What modules did you take in your first/second/third year?

- ✔ Why did you take those modules?

- ✔ What was your favourite module and why?

- ✔ How was the course assessed?

- ✔ What did you do for your final-year dissertation/project?

- ✔ What kind of contribution did you tend to make to seminars/tutorials?

- ✔ What did you do on your placement year? What did you learn from your experience?

- ✔ How would you rate the course overall? What was good about it and what could be improved?

Here's an example demonstrating a graduate's learning experiences:

More than anything, university has given me the skills to approach open-ended problems and evaluate how to tackle them. In approaching every assignment, I had to decide how much time to spend on it and what information I needed to gather before critically appraising the arguments and coming to my own conclusions.

Why did you choose to go to university as a mature student?

Ideally, aim to answer this question by focusing on the benefits to your personal or career development that you foresaw in gaining a degree.

This question is a great opportunity for you to demonstrate your commitment to your own personal development. So make sure that you inject plenty of energy and enthusiasm into your voice and body language when answering this question (see Chapter 3).

✔ *Basically, I thought it would be good for my personal development. I left school at the age of sixteen and while it never held me back in my career, I did start to wonder if further education may be good for me – in terms of giving me a broader perspective on how to analyse problems and critique arguments. And I've certainly gained that from the course.*

✔ *At the time, I had reached somewhat of a plateau in my career. You see a lot of job adverts for the more senior roles that talk about wanting degree-educated candidates. Also I thought that a degree may challenge me intellectually as well as give me a career kick-start. Certainly, I had been applying for management roles before my degree without much luck. But with the degree under my belt, I'm finding that employers – such as yourselves – are much more interested now.*

How difficult did you find university as a mature student?

The interviewers may be implying that your age or lack of practice at studying and revising for exams held you back from realising your full potential.

Mentioning that you found the return to study difficult initially is okay. But a good answer tells the interviewers how you overcame any initial difficulties.

> ✔ *I did find it difficult at first. I hadn't done any real studying and I certainly hadn't revised for an exam in over 12 years. However, I persisted and I'm ever so pleased that I got an upper second-class degree overall.*

> ✔ *I didn't really experience any particular difficulties to do with the studying itself. The main hardship was in juggling my full-time job with my part-time studies. On average I was doing ten hours of study a week on my own as well as attending lectures every third weekend. Studying has been hard, but it has been worth it in terms of the knowledge and wider understanding of my field that I've gained.*

You may be able to divert the interviewers by talking about the financial hardship of returning to full-time study and how you had to budget carefully in order to manage it.

How do you think your degree is relevant to this job?

This question is a more forthright version of *What have you learnt from being at university?* (dealt with earlier in this chapter). In answering the question, try to relate the skills from your degree to those necessary for the job.

Don't fall into the trap of talking about course content, as most interviewers will just start to glaze over!

> ✔ *I think my degree is very relevant because of the skills that I picked up. I spent most of the last three years researching*

for essays and discussion groups, so I learnt a lot about critically evaluating information and thinking about the best
way to present arguments.

✔ I feel that I have acquired transferable skills that will help
me to get on in this job. We worked mainly in teams, so I
have a good sense of how to negotiate with team members
and organise other people to get a project done on time.
And because we had a tight budget, we couldn't always do
what we initially wanted to do, so I've learnt a lot about
finding creative solutions to problems.

I don't see why someone with your degree would want to work in our field

Perhaps you read philosophy at university but now want to
work in investment banking. Maybe you studied physics but
now want to work in market research. Or your degree was in
art history but you decide to pursue a career in advertising.
Whatever the case, give a compelling reason to explain your
apparent change of direction.

Don't just talk about why you don't want to work in the field
related to your degree subject. Always go on to explain why
you do want to work in the interviewers' field.

✔ Despite having enjoyed my chemistry course, I have come to
realise over the last year that I don't want a career in chemical research. The pace of research – even in industry – is
relatively slow and the work can be quite solitary. I want a
career that's faster paced and more team-orientated. Added
to that, I've enjoyed the numerical side of my course – and
for those reasons I think finance would suit me.

✔ I chose to study French at university because it was my
favourite A Level. What I have enjoyed most in my degree
is the fact that I'm constantly communicating with people –
whether in writing or in person. It's important for me to find
a job that I can see myself progressing in for at least ten
years. And the fact that publishing is about communicating
and disseminating ideas to a wider audience is incredibly
appealing to me.

What sorts of part-time jobs have you had?

Students can't always pick and choose the jobs that they would like to do. Of course you may have gained relevant work experience, but the reality is that part-time jobs are more often about paying bills.

Don't just list the jobs that you had – explain why you took them too.

Consider these examples:

- ✔ *I worked in the students' union bar because I needed some way to avoid getting into too much debt during my course.*

- ✔ *In the summer holidays, I went home and took temping jobs in various local companies so that I could avoid having to take out any further student loans.*

- ✔ *I managed to get a job as a runner during the summer for the local radio station. It was unpaid, but I was glad to do it because I thought that getting some practical experience was more important than earning a couple of quid an hour working in a pub or an office.*

What did you learn from your part-time jobs?

Try relating some of the skills you acquired through your part-time work back to the job that you are applying for.

An alternative (and equally valid) tactic would be to talk about the lessons that you learned from your part-time work.

- ✔ *It helped me to develop my time management skills – in juggling 12 hours of bar work a week on top of my lectures and course work. But I was also made bar supervisor in my second year, so I'm unusual in that I'm a recent graduate with experience of managing other people.*

> ✔ *Working as a temp, I got to observe a lot of different company cultures and different managerial styles. Without mentioning any names, I came to appreciate how important having a supportive boss is. And I think I have a good grasp of what makes for effective team working too.*

What did you most enjoy about your time at university?

Foolish candidates may slip up by admitting that they most enjoyed the partying. A more canny answer to this question is to talk about how you enjoyed developing your skills.

Think about the nature of the job that you are being interviewed for. What skills would the interviewers be most interested in hearing you talk about?

> ✔ *I got the biggest buzz from working with others. I did enjoy researching assignments, but I looked forward most to tutorials and workshops in which we got to discuss our results and debate issues with class mates.*

> ✔ *My course taught me problem-solving skills. School had always been frustrating because it focused on learning information parrot-fashion. But I enjoyed my course because it was about facing problems and applying my creativity to finding solutions.*

What did you find the most difficult about your course?

Don't try to claim that nothing was difficult – the interviewers may think that you lack the ability to critically evaluate your own strengths and weaknesses.

A great answer is to say that you found some elements of the course difficult initially, but later developed your skills in those areas and have now conquered them.

> ✔ *In my first year, I didn't really enjoy the tutorials because I used to be quite a quiet individual when I was at school so I didn't feel comfortable speaking up. But over the course of three years, I got much more confident and now my*

tutor – who is one of my referees – describes me as a confident individual and a valued contributor to debates and discussions.

✔ *In my first few months, I used to struggle with time management. Assignments are so open-ended that I used to find it difficult to curtail my enthusiasm for a topic. But I quickly learned that I couldn't read round a topic endlessly. I needed to focus on gathering just enough information to produce a good assignment. So now I'm much more pragmatic in my approach to work.*

✔ *Having studied social science rather than science A Levels, I really hated the statistics to begin with. And my first-year results reflect that. But I was determined not to let it be my weak point so I bought some books on the subject and got some tutoring from a friend who was also doing a lot of stats on his course. And I'm pleased that I can now say that I'm as good a statistician as any of the other people who completed my course.*

What did you do outside of your studies?

Employers sometimes get it into their heads that students are lazy good-for-nothings, only interested in partying and sleeping in. Even if that description fits, you don't need me to tell you to avoid talking about those wilder aspects of your student life!

If you can, aim to talk about any extra-curricular activities you were involved in. Talk about your involvement in sports, committees, charities, societies, and community projects:

✔ *I was treasurer of our departmental society. I was elected into the post by the students in our year. As a member of the committee, I was responsible for helping to organise events such as the departmental fair for prospective students as well as the welcoming party for first-year students.*

✔ *I was very much involved with my hall of residence. We had various sports teams and I played on the rugby and cricket teams, which involved a weekly training session and matches about once every two weeks. In addition, I helped out with events at the hall of residence. For example, every time we had a themed party or ball, I would help with producing posters and selling tickets.*

Why have you left applying for jobs until after finishing your course?

Many candidates leave the job search until after their courses simply because they don't know what they want to do after university. However, a good answer focuses on the fact that delaying the job search is a deliberate decision on your part.

I realise that I missed the early round of recruitment, but I wanted to focus on getting the best possible degree class that I could. My thinking was that you only have one shot at getting a good degree. Since then, I have been able to focus fully on researching possible career choices and which the best companies are to work for. And this is what has brought me to apply to you.

Why did you choose to study part time rather than full time?

Perhaps you needed to earn a living or wanted to gain valuable work experience at the same time as studying.

Finish your answer by talking about the positive aspects of working at the same time as studying.

Having a mortgage, it was simply never an option to take three years out to study full time. But I'm glad that I continued to work at the same time because it helped me to focus on why I chose this degree, which was in order to help me in my chosen career.

Questions for School Leavers

A lot of interviewers are a bit fixated with wanting to employ graduates. So you need to prove that you are every bit as focused and able to weigh up options and make reasoned choices as people who did go on to university.

What subjects did you enjoy most?

Even though this question is about what subjects you enjoyed the most, you should focus the bulk of your answer on why particular subjects may be of use to the employer.

English and biology were my favourite subjects because I had really good teachers who made them enjoyable. But I think the most useful one is actually history. We had to do a lot of research and reading around different topics, which will stand me in good stead for this job.

What subjects were you good at?

Even though this sounds like a factual question, try to tweak your response so that you can explain why you think you should get the job (refer to Chapter 2 for a refresher on spotting the key skills interviewers look for).

I did well at maths and English. But we were not offered the opportunity to study art at school, which is where I feel that my true strengths and work ambitions lie.

What subjects were you not so good at?

Answer the question quickly – without dwelling on your weaknesses – but finish off by talking about some of your strengths instead:

✔ *I found maths difficult, because I struggled to get to grips with numbers in some of that very academic environment. But when I apply my maths skills to real life situations – for example when I'm cashing up in my Saturday job – I think that I'm actually quite good with numbers.*

✔ *Languages were not my strong suit. I was more interested in science and maths – both of which I passed with good grades.*

Avoid blaming the teachers for your poor performance, as this only reflects badly on you.

Never lie about your grades. If offered a job, you may be asked to bring your original examination certificates in so that the employer can check your qualifications.

Why didn't you stay on at school?

A good answer is to talk about wanting to join the workforce as quickly as possible.

I did consider staying on, but on reflection decided that further study wasn't really for me. My older brothers had both gone straight into work after finishing their GCSEs and are both doing very well in their jobs now. I've also taken the decision to start work because I want to earn a living for myself rather than have to be dependent on my family for a few more years.

You may want to finish off your answer by saying that you are open to the possibility of doing further study later on: *However, I do realise that I may need to pursue further qualifications at a later stage.*

Do you regret not staying on at school?

Even if you do regret not staying on at school, try not to dwell on the past. Instead, focus on what you have achieved.

No, I don't regret it at all. I was never academically gifted, but on joining the bank as a school leaver, I found a career that really played to my strengths. I have good communication and influencing skills – and those skills were simply not rewarded at school.

Another option is to talk about intending to continue with your education in the near future.

No, it was the right thing to do because I was itching to earn some money and get onto the career ladder. However, I'm certainly not against further education and intend to start a correspondence course in marketing in the next 12 to 18 months after I have settled into a new job – hopefully with you.

Why didn't you go to university?

Interviewers want to know that people who left school without going on to university did so because they decided it was the right option for them – and not simply because they did not get the grades or were not motivated enough to go on to further study:

> ✔ *I did think about going to university, but I knew that I wanted to learn on the job through practical application rather than study a subject in a largely theoretical manner.*

> ✔ *I would like to have had that option, but my financial circumstances at the time prevented me from being able to. I looked into how much it would cost me and because my parents were unable to offer me any additional support, I simply couldn't have afforded to do a full-time course. So I decided that I would work for a few years first. However, once I started work, I found that I was good at it and got promoted quickly.*

In retrospect, do you think you should have gone to university?

This question is very similar to 'Do you regret not staying on at school?' (covered earlier in this chapter). Focus on the future rather than mulling over the past.

It's difficult to say because you can never know exactly how it may have turned out. All I can say is that not having a degree has never held me back. I've been judged by results and as you will see from my CV, I was promoted to branch supervisor within two years. And then last year I was promoted to operations manager. Whereas if I'd gone to university, I'd only now be starting out as a trainee.

Mention that you are open-minded about the prospect of further education later on in your career.

I'm certainly not against the idea of further study and I'm cur-rently looking into doing an Open University diploma in psych-ology. Hopefully, if I enjoy that, then I can enroll on the full psychology degree. But at the time I left school, I'm glad that I did not go to university because I have gained some fantastic work experience that allows me to get more out of the further education that I eventually embark on.

What further education do you think you will need for this job?

In order to answer this question, you must research the nature of the job and the industry in order to find out what qualifications are necessary to get on.

Even if you don't intend to study for any qualifications soon, talk about your willingness to do them in the future.

Tailor the answer that is right for you based upon one of these examples:

✔ *I've been working as a child minder for three years now, so I guess the time is approaching for me to further my knowl-edge by pursuing an NVQ. A couple of my colleagues at my current nursery are doing it at the moment and seem to be getting a lot out of it.*

✔ *In order to progress, I need to deepen my understanding of international trade law. Whether I do a master's in the sub-ject or can learn enough about it on the job isn't immedi-ately apparent to me. However, it is certainly something that I will be looking further into once I have left my cur-rent company and settled into a new one.*

✔ *I know that I haven't had very much experience of market-ing or the public relations side of what we do. But rather than study a course or take exams on the subject, I think I would gain most by taking a placement or being seconded for a stint in a marketing department. Would that be an option if I were to join your business?*

Chapter 11

Handling Questions Aimed at Experienced Candidates

. . . .

In This Chapter

▶ Understanding the questions most typically aimed at older or more experienced candidates

▶ Explaining gaps and changes of career direction

▶ Giving employers good reason to let you return to work

. . . .

*A*s you get older and (hopefully!) wiser, you have more on your CV that interviewers may want you to talk about. Therefore in this chapter I focus specifically on questions asked of candidates with a few more years – and perhaps a couple more jobs – under their belts.

Questions for Older Candidates

Ageism is an unfortunate reality of recruitment, because interviewers often believe that younger candidates are more willing to work hard and are hungrier for success. As an older candidate, you must demonstrate – not only through your answers but also through the energy and enthusiasm that you put into your voice and body language – that you're just as committed and determined as the youngsters!

You may think that ageism only affects candidates in their fifties or even forties. However, a survey from just a few years ago showed that candidates as young as 35 were feeling discriminated against in the workplace.

How would you rate your progress so far?

The interviewers want you to talk about how fast you have risen up the ranks. They are trying to figure out whether your progress in the past may determine how hard-working you'll be in the future. Mention some of your career highlights to emphasise how pleased you are with your progress.

I've made good progress so far and hope to continue to make good progress in the near future too. I was promoted to project leader in January of last year and I've now worked on four lengthy projects involving large project teams of over a dozen people each time. But I think a lot of scope for growth still exists and that's partly what attracts me to the opportunity in your team.

If you feel that your progress has been somewhat slow compared to others in your peer group, explain why. Otherwise the interviewers may come to their own conclusion that you're looking for a job to pay the bills rather than because you want a new challenge and to make an impact on an organisation.

I think I've made good progress given the constraints of my current organisation. The company has been doing quite badly for a number of years and in retrospect I've probably stayed with it for too long out of a sense of loyalty. But I've now come to realise that I really need to move on because staying will have a negative effect on the rest of my career.

Do you feel that you should have achieved more in your current job?

If the interviewers spot that you were employed in one particular role for quite a long time, talk about some of the achievements that you were responsible for during that period.

I realise that I've had the same job title for over eight years, but the role has actually evolved substantially. The organisation has been through three restructurings in that time, and I've been heavily involved in initiating those change processes. My team has changed significantly, and I've been responsible for training them and seeing some of them move on to chunkier roles. I've also managed to reduce costs in my department by perhaps 20 to 30 per cent over that period.

Be incredibly careful about blaming your lack of progress on family circumstances or personal issues. Only do so if you can tell the interviewers that those issues have now completely gone away.

I could probably have done more in that role. But at the time we had two young children so it suited me just for those few years to have a steady job rather than a massively challenging one. But now that the children are older, I'm looking to throw myself completely into my career again and find a job that will give me a fresh challenge.

I'm concerned because you've been with one employer for a very long time – why is that?

The interviewers may be worried that your length of service with one organisation has made you set in your ways. Your answer needs to convince them that you are looking forward to the challenge of coping with a new culture and getting to grips with unfamiliar rules and regulations, processes, and procedures.

Respond to the interviewers' concerns by giving examples of how you have adapted to new circumstances and situations within your organisation.

I had no reason to leave for a long time. I was enjoying working within the organisation and felt that I was learning a lot. The team was growing in size and my responsibilities were constantly expanding. To put my progress in perspective, I joined as a clerk and I'm now an executive sitting on the regional management team. Only recently have I thought about moving jobs because the market has continued to evolve and our organisation has not. I can foresee a day when players in the market such as your organisation will overtake us.

The changing face of employment

The working environment has changed dramatically in the last few decades. The previous generation of employees anticipated joining one company and working their way up within that organisation. Employees expected their employer to look after them and provide them with training and promotions until they retired. In return, employees were expected to give the organisation their total loyalty. A 'job for life' was the norm.

However, those days are gone. In an age of redundancies, downsizing, and cost-cutting programmes, employees can find themselves without a job at very short notice. And, unfortunately, having had one employer for your entire career often does count against you. So you need to look after your own career and ensure that you remain employable. Recruiters advise people in their twenties and thirties to change employers approximately every three to five years to avoid struggling to find a new job post-redundancy.

This is a challenging role – are you sure you want to take it on at this stage of your career?

The law prevents interviewers from discriminating openly against older candidates – but this question is essentially asking you: *Are you too old to do this job?*

Chapter 13 deals with tackling illegal and personal questions, and you can find more information on age discrimination in Liz Barclay's *Small Business Employment Law For Dummies* (Wiley).

Aim to impress the interviewers by talking about the goals you have yet to attain.

> ✔ *Yes, very much so. I am now human resources director of one of the largest business units in the company. However, the role of group human resources director of an international business has always been my goal. And this opportunity with you will help me with that career path.*

> ✔ *I still feel that there's still so much to learn and I hate the idea of allowing myself to stagnate. Medical advancements mean that our profession has changed so much and it continues to change. Learning new methods and techniques still gives me a kick and I'm hoping that the better resources at your hospital will give me exposure to an even broader range of cases .*

How have you changed in the last ten years?

Employers want to hire people who open themselves to new experiences and adapt to change. Answer this question by giving a concrete example of how you have changed.

Focus on the positive ways in which you have changed rather than the negative!

I had a quick temper when I was younger. But as the years have gone by and I've moved into management, I've learnt to control my irritation and now I can take a much more dispassionate view of problems. By staying calm, I can think more clearly and weigh up the different options for handling the situation. I'm amazed by my previous anger levels, as I now realise that shouting and screaming are pointless when the most important thing is to sort the issue out.

Interviewers can easily ask about any time frame. So be ready to tailor your response should the interviewers ask you how you have changed over – for example – five, a dozen, or twenty years.

When do you plan to retire?

This may sound like a strange question to ask. But given that you are not required to put your age on your CV, interviewers may not know how old you are. Employers like to feel they are getting value out of the people they hire. Certainly, for senior posts, employers may have to pay hefty fees to headhunters or recruitment consultants in order to take you on. Strictly speaking, this isn't an illegal question as the employer only wants to check that you aren't planning on retiring almost as soon as you have started the job.

The best answer to this question is to say that you're not intending to retire for at least five years. But if you are unable to say that truthfully, make sure that you emphasise the value you'll contribute in your short time with the organisation.

Ideally I'm not looking to retire for quite a few years yet. I'm 62 next year but I plan to work on longer than 65 as I still find the work so stimulating. Neither does it mean I'm ready to take a job and sit on my behind for that period. I'm still very much committed to the job and want to make a major contribution to a team before I retire. I wouldn't be looking for a new job if I simply wanted to take it easy for the next few years.

Talking about Changes of Direction in Your CV

Employers are often scared of taking risks. For this reason, they usually prefer to take on candidates who have run-of-the-mill backgrounds – people who have worked their way up in the one industry. For many employers, candidates with an unusual background scare employers a little.

If you have a career including any significant changes of direction, work hard to convince the interviewers that you really are the best person for the job.

Why have you changed jobs so many times?

The interviewers are probably implying that if you've switched jobs frequently in the past, are you likely to move on from theirs sometime soon as well? Whatever reasons you give for your changing jobs in the past, aim to assure the interviewers that your circumstances have now completely changed.

To add the icing to the cake, finish your response with a compelling reason why you intend to make this next career move your last one – for quite a few years anyway.

After citing your reasons, offer a finishing statement along the lines of:

My work has always been a big part of who I am. And having researched your company and customers and having met a few of you now, I think this could be a place where I could learn and grow in a role.

Avoid blaming job moves on interpersonal difficulties. Mentioning this reason once may be acceptable, but mentioning it more times signals to interviewers that you're difficult to manage.

Take a look at these two examples:

> ✔ *I really enjoy the job, but haven't had much luck finding an employer that fits me. My first company suffered financial problems and made several of us redundant. I left the next company because they wouldn't support me in my professional exams. My next employer got taken over and a round of redundancies occurred. And in my current organisation, I feel like an insignificant cog in a massive machine given their huge size. What I want to do is find a medium-sized business, like yours, which is small enough for me to get to know the whole team well, but at the same time large enough to offer me some variety in my work.*

> ✔ *I moved around a couple of times because I was essentially pretty immature and wasn't very focused on my career. In my early twenties I didn't have much direction. But that drifting is all in the past – I got married a couple of years ago and have very different priorities now. As you can see, I've been with my current employer for nearly two years and am only considering your company because you are offering more responsibility in the role.*

In the first example, the candidate gives a compelling reason (wanting to move into a medium-sized business) for wanting to move this one last time. In the second example, the candidate uses marriage as a way of drawing a line between a flighty past and a career-oriented future.

You may find it difficult to talk about why you moved from job to job, as any reasons can sound a little negative. So conveying your passion for the job is doubly important (see Chapter 3 for more on putting across emotions through your voice and body language).

Given your background, why have you decided to change career?

Are you an accountant who wants to become a teacher, an IT engineer who wants to become a gym instructor, or a surveyor who now wants to train as a physiotherapist? Whatever your choice, work hard to convince the interviewer to take you on at the start of a drastic career change.

Mention some of your transferable skills from your previous roles or your more relevant experience and relate them to your new chosen career. If you're lacking relevant skills to talk about, see the sidebar 'Getting the right experience' for ideas to help you out.

> ✔ *Realising what I really wanted to do took me a while. I've been flitting around between various corporate jobs for seven years now and I've certainly enjoyed most of them. But I've come to the realisation that I definitely don't want to be confined to an office. Then I hit upon the idea of nursing – a profession that allows me plenty of people contact outside of an office environment. In the last year, I've been doing some voluntary work on Saturday mornings at a local hospice and that experience has totally cemented the idea that I want to take up nursing as a vocation.*

> ✔ *I started working in hospitality in various hotel and restaurant jobs. But then I wanted to travel so went to work for an airline. Now I've decided that I want a stable career that doesn't involve shifts. Little opportunity exists for career progression in hospitality or the airlines. For this reason, I'm looking to join your organisation – because you're offering a training programme plus a more stable working environment that will enable me to grow and progress in a career. However, all of my roles have involved considerable customer contact, so I have a good understanding of what makes people tick and how to deal with them, which I think is essential in working for a bank.*

Getting the right experience

Changing careers can be a bit of a chicken and egg situation. Employers won't take a risk on you because you don't have the right skills and experience; at the same time, you can't get the right skills and experience because no one gives you the chance!

Voluntary work is one of the best ways to develop your skills and experience. Volunteering for a few evenings or weekends a month can often be a stepping-stone to getting the job that you ultimately want.

Approach organisations such as:

✔ Charities, welfare groups, local schools, and homes for the sick or elderly.

✔ Hospitals or hospital radio stations.

✔ Environmental and conservation groups.

✔ Political parties, arts centres, and churches.

Volunteers can get involved in all manner of activities, from fund-raising to working in a charity shop, handling back office paperwork to working on projects in the community. You can get more information about volunteering from Web sites, including:

✔ www.volunteering.org.uk

✔ www.csv.org.uk

✔ www.vso.org.uk

Do you want to change career because you are disillusioned with your current one?

This is a negatively phrased question. The interviewers are implying that you are running away from your current or last career rather than looking to change into a new career for positive reasons.

Avoid going into detail about the reasons you are disillusioned with your current or last career. Focus instead on the positive reasons that attract you to your new career. No one likes a moaner!

Yes, I have been feeling less motivated about my current role. But I've been giving the issue a lot of thought and have decided that this change of career is right for me. Just like a lot of other people, I ended up in my current career rather than planned it. Now, however, I am making a conscious plan. This job is right for me because I think consultancy will give me exposure to a wide range of businesses across industry sectors. In addition, the projects will tend to be shorter and more challenging – so a steeper learning curve will exist and I'll learn more as a result.

To what extent are your personal circumstances impacting upon your desire to change career?

Perhaps you mentioned earlier in your interview that you're moving in with your partner, having children, or getting divorced. If the interviewers are asking you this question, they may be worried that your desire to change career is because you are looking for an easier life or because you're running away from your old life.

Avoid getting into detail about your personal life. Instead, reassure the interviewers that your sitting in this interview is a reasoned and rational decision on your part.

Note that in both of these two example responses, the candidates tell the interviewers that they have rationally evaluated the impact of their personal lives on their work:

> ✔ *I can honestly say that starting a family has very little to do with my desire to change careers. In fact, doing this job will mean taking a cut in my salary – at a time when the additional family member means that we'll need more money. But I just can't give up this opportunity to move into a creative field.*

> ✔ *Perhaps getting divorced has made me look at all aspects of my life again. But I've been very careful to separate the emotional changes in my life from the rational decisions that I need to make about my career.*

Only allow yourself to talk about your personal circumstances if they directly relate to your new career.

I'd say that my personal circumstances are very relevant to my choice to train as an acupuncturist. I was in such a poor state of health before I started seeing an acupuncturist myself. I was totally amazed at the improvement in wellbeing that I experienced in only six sessions. So I began looking into Chinese medicine and alternative health models. I've been reading extensively around the topic for some time now. But what sealed this choice of career for me was meeting different practising acupuncturists and getting a feel for how they spend their time and how rewarding they find it.

How do we know that you'll stick with this change of direction?

This is a perfectly valid question. If you're dissatisfied with what you've been doing up until now, how do the interviewers know that you won't get dissatisfied with this new career too?

Try to convince the interviewers that this is what you want to do by talking about the time, effort, and money you have invested in researching and educating yourself about your new career.

Don't forget that interviewers are not only evaluating *what* you say but also *how* you say it. If you don't sound enthusiastic and passionate about your new career choice, why should the interviewers believe you?

The following examples demonstrate your research (in the first example), and your passion (in the second):

> ✔ *I'm going to stick with a career this time because I've always had a passion for property. I read about property trends in the papers and on Web sites and talk about property with friends. Over the last few months, I've also sought out different estate agents to find out the precise ins and outs of the job. I feel that I have an excellent appreciation of the realities of the job. I understand that the hours can be very long and that my pay will be almost totally dependent on my performance, but those details don't put me off – in fact I feel even more determined to work in the industry.*

✔ All of my jobs so far have helped me understand what I enjoy about working life. I started in finance but found that I didn't get enough people contact. I moved into human resources but felt my organisation wasn't taking our department seriously enough, so I switched to sales admin. Through working with the sales people and getting to know them and learn exactly what they do, I realised that I wanted to work in sales too. This job has the perfect combination of features for me – I enjoy being with people, and using my brain to figure out how to influence them. I can guarantee you that this is the job I have always been looking for.

How do you feel about starting at the bottom again?

Don't reply to this question by just saying that starting over at the bottom isn't an issue. You need to demonstrate to the interviewers that you have given this situation some thought.

Getting an insight into your new career

Changing career can be incredibly daunting. Talking to people who are already in your dream job is one of the best ways to find out whether your new career is really going to suit you.

If you don't know anyone who works in your chosen field, then ask round. Talk to your friends and family – do they know anyone who is in your dream job?

Once you find a contact, arrange a chat over coffee – and of course you buy!

Good questions to ask people already in the job include:

✔ What do they do on a day-to-day, hour-by-hour basis? What do they most enjoy about their work? What are the worst or most boring aspects of the job?

✔ What career paths exist in the industry? Do people in the profession tend to be self-employed or set up their own business? Or do they join small, medium, or large organisations?

✔ What training did they require? What exams or other forms of assessment did they have to complete? How expensive was the course?

I think I'm going to enjoy the situation actually. I'd be a fool to expect to come into your industry without any relevant experience. I know that the first six months is filled mainly with running errands and doing other people's administration. But the whole point of being a runner is to absorb information and learn, and that's exactly what I'll be doing for the first year.

How will you cope working with peers who are ten years younger than you?

This question is a variation on the preceding one, 'How do you feel about having to start at the bottom again?'. You need to convince the interviewers that this concern is not an issue.

If you have any younger peers or perhaps a younger manager in your current job, mention this in support of your answer that this issue won't be a problem for you.

I don't think it will be an issue at all. In my current job, a few of the managers at my level are a good few years younger than me anyway and we all get on very well. And the fact that I'll be working with lots of enthusiastic younger people will keep me on my toes.

How will you cope with the drop in salary that changing career necessitates?

In answering this question, you need to convince the interviewers that you have weighed up the pros and cons – and decided that the pros ultimately outweigh the cons.

I've given a lot of thought to this issue. But I've wanted a job in this field for so many years now that I must simply cut back to make this work. I've already calculated exactly how much I need to live on and where I can save. But in the longer term, my firm intention is to work my way up in this industry, so earning the entry-level salary for the rest of my life is unlikely.

If you have a partner at home who's willing to shoulder some of your financial commitments, then do tell the interviewers.

Although an interviewer should not ask about your home or personal life, you may choose to bring it up yourself if you think that doing so is an asset in the interview. Strictly speaking, the interviewers shouldn't ask you further questions about your partner. But in reality their curiosity may get the better of them. So do be ready to answer a few conversational questions about your partner if you mention them first!

What would you do if you were unable to secure a job in this profession?

This question is a test of how much you want to change careers and enter the interviewers' profession. Are you completely dedicated to this one profession?

Get across the fact that you are only looking for jobs in this particular field.

I'd be devastated if I couldn't work in this profession as I've set my heart on doing so. But to be honest, I'm not considering the possibility of failure at the moment. Your company is obviously one of the top-rated organisations in this field. But if I fail to impress you, I will continue to apply for jobs with some of the lesser-known organisations.

Returning to Work

Interviewers worry about candidates who have taken – or been forced to take – any length of time out from work. Their biggest worry is that being out of employment may make you lazy and reluctant to engage in hard work.

Embellish on your past or covering up the cracks with a few lies may be very, very tempting – but remember that potential employers often check references. So be careful not to get caught out telling porky pies!

You have a gap in your CV – what did you do in that time?

Answer this question by focusing on the positive ways in which you spent your time. Perhaps you took time out to travel, do a course, or pick up a new skill. Maybe you were nursing a sick family member back to health. Or you may have been spending a lot of time researching a new career and looking for a new job.

Whatever you plan to say, convince the employers that you weren't merely sitting around watching daytime telly!

Consider these alternative responses:

- ✔ *When I was made redundant, I saw it as an opportunity to take some time out. I took three months off to travel through South America. And then I spent another two months renovating the old house that we bought but have never had the time to do up. Having taken this career break, I'm now completely refreshed and ready to return to full-time employment*

- ✔ *Unfortunately my partner became ill. The doctor said that my partner would need full time care. And because I wasn't willing to consider a care home, I decided to provide the care myself. My last employer wasn't willing to hold my position open indefinitely so I had to quit. Thankfully, my partner is now on the mend so I can think about returning to work and frankly I'm looking forward to it.*

Are you concerned that your time away from the workforce may put you at a disadvantage?

This question is a more upfront variant of 'You have a gap in your CV – what did you do in that time?' (see the preceding question). Your tactic should be to convince the interviewers that you have been spending your time engaging in relevant activities.

This question is phrased quite aggressively. In fact, the interviewers may be asking this question to see if you react in a hostile fashion. Don't take the bait – stay calm.

I can understand your concern, but I can assure you that I've not been sitting around doing nothing. Looking for a job is a full-time job in itself, and I initially spent a lot of time registering with agencies and researching options. When it became obvious that a job would not be forthcoming immediately, I decided to look for a way to occupy my time and keep my brain ticking over. So now I'm spending two days a week doing some voluntary work raising funds for a local charity for stray dogs.

Why did your last employer select you for redundancy?

Redundancy used to carry much more of a stigma than it does in the modern workplace. In an age of cost-cutting and downsizing programmes, redundancy is now merely a reality of working life.

If you can, explain that your redundancy was a cost-saving decision taken by the management rather than a personal decision because they didn't like you!

Actually, about 30 of us were chosen for redundancy purely because we were the most junior staff. When the business started to do badly, they made a decision to reduce the size of our department by 15 per cent. Unfortunately, I was one of that percentage.

Talking about how your role was made redundant by a restructuring in the team is an alternative response to this question.

You may naturally feel hurt to have been made redundant. But avoid taking your feelings out on your former managers by talking disparagingly of them, as doing so may backfire and reflect badly on you.

Have you ever been fired?

'No' is the only safe answer to this question. But if you can't honestly answer 'no', then think through exactly how you want to explain your circumstances.

No, I've never been fired. I was made redundant from my previous job because the German business that bought us out wanted to reduce the size of the Birmingham office. But that was a business decision that affected several of us rather than a firing because of anything I had done.

Be careful not to lie – especially if you have been fired from your most recent job. Employers usually make job offers *subject to references* (meaning they offer you the job but reserve the right to withdraw it if your referees don't paint a pretty picture of your working life). And if you have been fired, your last boss is almost certain to mention this fact in writing your reference.

I'm afraid to say that I was fired from my last job. But in retrospect it wasn't the right career move for me and I should never have taken the job. I took the position because it was offering a much bigger salary. But making cold calls and selling to customers really doesn't play to my strengths. I was repeatedly missing targets and my boss did talk to me a couple of times. I was getting very despondent and when he eventually fired me, I was honestly glad to get out. But the upshot of that dismissal is that I can now focus on getting a job that does utilise my skills – and so all of my job applications now are in the field of sales support rather than sales itself.

Why have you been out of work for so long?

You must be able to account for your time off. Begin your answer by talking about the steps that you have taken to try to find a job. And finish off by talking about having rejected other options because you are keen to find exactly the right type of organisation to work for.

I'm looking for a very particular type of job. The position needs to be part time so that I can juggle my family commitments. In addition, I don't have a car at the moment so I'm looking for less than 45 minutes' travelling time either way. On top of that, I want a job that will provide some training and opportunities to grow. Not many jobs fulfil all of those criteria – but thankfully yours does, which is why I'm so glad that you invited me to this interview today.

Do mention if you have been offered any jobs, as this enhances your desirability in the eyes of the interviewers.

I have been spending the time looking for a job. But finding the right job is important to me. I was offered a marketing role about two months ago. But after some hard thinking, I decided to decline the offer because it wasn't quite right for me. That company works in the business-to-business market whereas I'm now certain that it's the business-to-consumer market that I can get most enthused about.

If you hadn't been made redundant, would you have considered work in this field?

A lot of people see redundancy as an opportunity to retrain in a new profession. When giving your answer, focus mainly on what draws you to your new career rather than dwelling on your redundancy and the past.

Spend no more than a single sentence talking about the past and the redundancy. Apart from your one sentence to acknowledge that this is a question about career change, answer it as if the interviewers have asked you *Why do you want to work in this field?*

Perhaps I wouldn't have considered working in this field. But I've had a lot of time to think about and research new careers. And I've come to the conclusion that becoming a clinic technician is the right job for me. The fact that I'm going to be spending the majority of my day on my feet with patients is perfect as I'd much rather be with people than sat in an office. I also enjoy learning and keeping up with technical developments, so that part of the job requirement suits me down to the ground too.

You've been working for yourself for some time now. Why do you want to work for someone else again?

Many employees talk about wanting to quit so that they can go into business working for themselves. So you can understand why interviewers may wonder why you want to throw yourself back into the rat race. Interviewers are often most concerned that you're only looking to become an employee again because you were unable to make a decent living as a self-employee.

Talk about the positive reasons you want to join an employer rather than the negative reasons you are looking to flee the world of self-employment.

Here are three example reasons:

- ✔ *I've enjoyed my 18 months working freelance. But my biggest concern when I set up on my own was always that I would miss the people interaction. And that prediction has come true. I want to have a team around me again as that's how I enjoy my work most and get my best work done.*

- ✔ *I enjoy the core activity of being a designer. But I found that I was spending too much of my time engaging in non-core activities such as networking and trying to find new clients, and then having to do the accounts, send out invoices, and chase payments. I've come to realise that I'd rather focus on being a designer and let other people take care of the financial and administrative sides of the business.*

- ✔ *The main reason I'm keen to return to work for a company is that I've been missing getting involved in large projects. Working for myself, I've tended to focus on smaller assignments and they've been fun for a while. But it's the large projects with big clients that will develop my skills and challenge me – and that's what I hope the return to employment will bring.*

Chapter 12

Handling Hypothetical and Analytical Questions

. . . .

In This Chapter

▶ Judging the best response to give to hypothetical questions

▶ Talking about key concepts

▶ Finding the solution to numerical questions

. . . .

*W*hile interviewers are interested in your past and the skills that you can bring to the job, they also want to know how well you may fit into their organisation. Having certain skills is all very well, but can you exercise them in any situation? So interviewers may ask hypothetical questions to gauge how you would deal with situations that they can foresee happening. If you're being interviewed for a management position, interviewers may also ask you to define key management concepts to see if you think along the same lines as they do.

If you are being interviewed for a job that requires a fair degree of ability with numbers, be ready to show you can analyse simple numerical problems and give the interviewer an answer. More often than not, interviewers expect you to handle these problems in your head rather than by using a calculator or even a pen and paper.

In this chapter, I discuss ways to deal with some of the most common hypothetical questions, and questions requiring definitions of management concepts. And I round off by giving you some examples of the most common numerical questions that interviewers are likely to pose.

Responding to Hypothetical Questions

Hypothetical questions almost always have the word 'would' in them. Look out for phrases such as *How would you...?* or *What would you...?* Another common tactic is to ask, *If ...blah blah blah. What would you do?*

Don't assume that a single right answer exists. Interviewers in a small, cost-conscious business may be looking for a very different answer to interviewers in a large, growing, and very successful company. Do your research and devise responses to the following hypothetical questions for each interview that you go to.

The secret to handling hypothetical questions is telling the interviewers what you think they want to hear – which may sometimes be different from what you would actually do.

What would you do if your boss asked you to do something that went against your principles?

Most people would probably answer this question by saying that it depends on what your boss had asked you to do. But 'it depends' is not a satisfactory answer. Tell the interviewers what they probably want to hear – that you would act in the best interests of the organisation.

This is a hypothetical situation. Even if in reality you are prepared to stand up for your principles, the interviewers would probably rather know that you would do what is best for their organisation.

The first thing to do is to weigh up the request against the values and rules of the organisation. If my boss has asked me to do something that is in line with those values but just goes against my personal values, I would have to do it anyway – because it is for the good of the organisation. However, if my boss has asked me to do something that is not in keeping with the organisation's values, then I would question it.

What would you do if you disagreed with a decision taken by your manager?

This is a similar question to the one above, so a similar tactic is probably a safe bet. Emphasise that you would try to discuss the decision with your manager first.

In preparing a response to this question, think about the nature of the interviewers' organisation. Do you think they would consider it most important to obey your manager? Or would they want you to act in the best interests of the organisation?

Contrast these two responses:

> ✔ *How I behave would depend on why I disagreed with the decision. For example, if I thought that the decision was not in the best interests of the organisation, then I would raise the issue with my manager and try to convince him or her of my arguments. If my manager listens to me and understands my reasons, but still wants to go ahead with his or her decision, then I would have to abide by it.*

> ✔ *If I thought that a decision would go against the interests of our organisation and our customers, then I would have to challenge my manager on the issue. If my manager did not see reason, then I may talk to a colleague and get a second opinion. If, on discussion, we felt that the decision was completely inappropriate – perhaps because it would damage the organisation or harm our relationships with customers – then I would have to escalate the issue and perhaps raise my concerns with my manager's manager.*

The second answer is more appropriate for situations in which you think your manager is clearly wrong. The first answer may be more appropriate if the decision is merely about a difference of opinion.

What would you do if your child were suddenly taken ill?

This question is rather unfair – potentially illegal – especially as it tends to be aimed at women with children rather than men (see Chapter 13 for more on illegal questions). As such, you may be technically within your rights to refuse to answer it. However, refusing to answer it can make you appear unnecessarily testy or aggressive. So try to keep any irritation in check.

Remember that this question relates to a purely hypothetical situation. In reality you may want to drop everything and head home to look after your child. But that answer won't get you the job.

Nurseries and day centres typically ask parents to remove their children if they have any illnesses that can infect other children. A good response to this question is saying that you have other people to look after your child if necessary.

> ✔ *My son is at a full-time nursery. But in case of medical emergencies, they have the contact details of my mother as well as my partner's parents. So one set of his grandparents would be more than happy to look after him. And certainly my parents nursed me and my siblings through everything from the measles to chickenpox.*

> ✔ *I have a very good nanny who looks after the children. So I'm sure that she would be able to cope with any minor medical emergencies – certainly most common childhood ailments and even a broken bone. It would have to be a very major emergency for me to have to go home – and I don't foresee that happening.*

Would you rather be a big fish in a small pond or a small fish in a big pond?

The 'right' answer to this question depends entirely on the size of the company that you are applying for. Read the organisation's literature carefully to work out how many people are employed – is it counted in dozens, hundreds, or thousands?

Interviewers can also ask you much more direct questions such as: *Why would you want to work for a small organisation like ours?* or *Why are you looking to join a large company when all of your experience so far has been with smaller ones?*

Compare or contrast your past experience of working in larger or smaller firms to what's on offer in each particular interview.

Take a look at these two different responses:

> ✔ *I'd much rather be a big fish in a small pond. Working in my current firm, with nearly 800 other lawyers, I feel that I have very little impact on the overall running of the business. I want to join a firm in which I can get to know the team better and feel that I am having more of a say in shaping its future.*

> ✔ *I'm looking to jump into a bigger pond. One of the main reasons I'm looking to join your organisation is that so far I have only worked for small companies. Joining a large business will give me exposure to larger and more complex projects across a number of offices and locations. Working in a large organisation will also give me a greater understanding of more sophisticated, leading-edge processes, too.*

If you spotted a colleague doing something unethical, what would you do?

In most instances, in response to this question the interviewers want you to say that you would take a course of action to intervene or report the person as appropriate. If there are certain 'right' ways of acting in your particular industry – for example, the legal and medical professions have very clear guidelines on how to deal with such individuals – then make sure your answer includes these.

I would get in touch with the human resources department to speak about the matter. I would try to discuss the issue confidentially and without mentioning the individual's name. If it became clear that his behaviour was definitely unethical, then I would report the issue to my line manager.

If you have dealt with this situation before, give this as an example. Examples are more credible than merely saying what you *would* do in this situation.

What would you do if a colleague came to you in tears?

Empathy and consideration for others are important qualities in employees. The worst thing in a crisis situation is having a colleague point the finger of blame or simply say *I told you so.*

Show the interviewers you have good listening skills and can offer not only practical assistance but also a shoulder to cry on.

I'd take my colleague aside – perhaps to an unoccupied office – and try to find out what had upset them. But to start with, the colleague probably doesn't want to be bombarded with questions, so I'd try to be sympathetic. Once they have calmed down, I would try to find out what the matter was. Then I would look for ways to help – such as taking on some of their work, talking to a difficult customer, or getting another colleague involved. But throughout, I'd focus on being sympathetic and reassuring.

How would you react if your boss said that you needed to come into the office for the entire weekend?

In practice, you may be a bit disgruntled about working at the weekend. But your response to this question needs to demonstrate your flexibility and commitment to the job.

Obviously, working at the weekend is not a situation that I hope will happen very often. But I'd have no problem with it. In fact, one of the reasons I'm looking to change jobs is because I'm starting to feel that my current role isn't sufficiently challenging – I'm being under-utilised. So in fact it may be a nice change to have too much work to do!

Talking about how you *would* react is all very well, but also try to give the interviewers an example of when you had to work outside your contracted hours.

Working hours are becoming an increasingly difficult area of working life. If you need some help in finding out what's legal and what's not, read Liz Barclay's *Small Business Employment Law For Dummies* (Wiley).

What would you say if I were to offer you this job right now?

The 'right' answer depends on how much the interviewers expect you to know about the job. For example, if you have been headhunted for a specific role and know relatively little about a post, then you can say:

Well, it sounds very interesting so far. But before accepting the job, I'd need to spend a bit more time researching the business and reading up on your products and the challenges ahead of you. Ideally I'd like to meet a few more of the team to find out whether we'd get on together. But so far it all sounds very promising.

If, however, the interviewers provide you with plenty of information about their organisation, the role, the salary and benefits, and you still want the job, then a better answer is to declare your enthusiasm:

I would say yes immediately. I've done a lot of reading about your organisation and I think that your positioning with regards to your competitors is fascinating. I also like the fact that this interview has been quite relaxed yet challenging. For me, that's a sign that this is the right place for me to work.

Defining Key Concepts

A little knowledge can be a dangerous thing. Sometimes interviewers who have read a management textbook or two may want to know whether you have the same level of insight into models and concepts as they do.

How would you define team work?

In asking this question, the interviewers want to know whether you can put the needs of the team ahead of your own needs.

Two common variations on this question are: *What makes for good team work?* and *How would you define co-operation?*

I would define team work as the ability for a group of individuals working together to accomplish more than they could accomplish individually. In practical terms, this means that individuals must be willing to put the needs of the team above their own needs at times.

Be ready to give an example of a time you demonstrated good teamworking skills, as the interviewers can easily follow up this question by asking: *And can you tell us about a time when you demonstrated your teamworking skills?*

What makes for a good working environment?

Answering this question requires a good idea of the kind of culture that typifies this industry or even this specific company. For example, interviewers in a public sector organisation may be looking for an answer that mentions the need to follow established rules, while a pharmaceutical company may expect candidates to talk about the need for people to have a thirst for knowledge.

Good research pays off in answering this type of question. Read widely to get an idea of the culture and kind of team environment within the interviewers' organisation. If, however, you're not sure of the working culture, talk briefly about some general features that all organisations aspire to:

I think it's really important for everyone to feel that they can express their opinions openly. Managers must be willing to listen to ideas and encourage everyone to pull together in the best interests of the team.

How would you define leadership?

Hundreds of definitions of leadership exist, so feel free to adopt one you already know. However, how you respond to this question may depend on the nature of the organisation interviewing you.

For example, a traditional organisation may expect an answer along these lines:

Leadership is about communicating the goals of the organisation to the team and then delegating tasks to appropriate members of the team, checking up on their work, and ensuring that they're making progress.

Alternatively, a more progressive organisation may want to hear about terms such as 'vision' and 'empowerment':

Leadership is about involving stakeholders to create a shared vision, and then motivating and empowering the team so that they want to achieve that vision. Good leadership is about getting to understand the strengths, weaknesses, and needs of individual members of the team and being able to coach and develop them so that they can tackle progressively greater problems and opportunities.

Dealing Effectively with Numerical Challenges

Employers often complain that employees lack ability with numbers. Most employees rely on calculators, cash tills, and computers for the most simple of numerical tasks. But what happens if you input the data wrongly and get a key decimal point in the wrong place? Or what if the cash till breaks down? The interviewers want to know whether you can cope without the benefit of technology.

How many bottles of carbonated water are consumed daily in California?

On the face of it, this question seems impossible to answer. How the heck should you know how many bottles are consumed daily in Britain – let alone California?

But the interviewers are not looking for a correct answer. They may not even know the precise answer themselves! Instead, what the interviewers are looking for is whether you can take a problem and, using reasonable assumptions and some mental arithmetic, come up with a sensible estimate.

A correct answer to numerical hypothetical questions rarely exists. Extrapolate from information that you do possess to calculate your estimate. As you may imagine, management consulting firms and investment banks, in particular, like to use these sorts of 'guesstimate' questions.

The answer to this question may go along these lines:

I've read somewhere that if California were a country in its own right, it would be something like the sixth or seventh largest country in the world. On the other hand, it's not as densely populated as most European countries, so I'd hazard a guess that it has only a tenth of the population of the UK or France, so it would have around five million people living there.

Thinking about the people that I know, I'd say that a lot of middle class people are drinking bottled water – so maybe one in three people in the UK drinks a bottle of water a day. But the question was about carbonated water. As most people seem to drink still water rather than fizzy, I'd estimate that only one in four bottles of water are carbonated. So that means that around one in twelve people in the UK drinks a bottle of carbonated water daily.

But people in California are reputedly much more health-conscious than those in the UK. So let's say twice as many people there drink bottled water. So that makes one in six people in California. So one in six out of five million people – that's, um . . . Well, one in five would be one million. So one in six is going to be around 850,000 people. So the answer is around 850,000 bottles of carbonated water a day.

In this example and those following, whether the number is 'correct' or not isn't the point. Rather, the assumptions, estimates, and mental calculations must seem reasonable – and these are more interesting to the interviewers than the actual answer itself.

 Talk out loud as you work out your answer. The interviewers don't want you to sit in silence calculating the answer and then simply say '60,000 bottles a day' at the end – they want to hear your chain of thought.

How many cars does Pakistan have?

This is another 'guesstimate' question. Again, the interviewers are interested in your line of reasoning. You may start this challenge by working out the population of Pakistan based on your general knowledge of the world, and then try to estimate how many people will own cars.

Remember, to talk through your assumptions out loud.

I think I read that India is the second largest country in the world, with a population of around 800 million people. From maps that I've seen of that part of the world, Pakistan is roughly a fifth or sixth of its size. Assuming it has a similar population density to India, let's call that 150 million people in Pakistan.

Now, large parts of the population are very poor, so won't have a car. I'd assume that around 90 per cent of the population are too poor to own a car. So that leaves 15 million people as potential car owners. Let's assume that each family only has one car.

In the UK, the typical family consists of two parents and 2.4 children. But in Asia, grandparents tend to live with families. And Asian countries have a higher birth rate, so let's call that three children. Assuming that there are seven or eight people in the average Pakistani family, that's 15 million divided by seven or eight which is . . . around two million cars?

I have a dinosaur on an island – how many sheep would I need on the island to feed it in perpetuity?

This is yet another 'guesstimate' question – although it is dressed up as a more complex problem. As dinosaurs died out millions of years before sheep lived on the planet, there really is no right answer to this question! Again, you need to make a number of reasonable assumptions and then arrive at an answer. By the way, I have heard an interviewer at a top investment bank ask candidates this question – I'm not making it up!

So the question is basically how many sheep would I need on the island in order for them to be able to breed enough to feed the dinosaur. Okay, let's assume that a meat-eating dinosaur needs to eat hundreds of kilograms of flesh every day – so let's call it 20 sheep every single day. Multiplying that number by 365 equals about 7000 sheep every year.

Now let's think about the rate at which sheep can breed. One ram can impregnate many dozens of female sheep, so let's assume that the population is 99 per cent female. I assume that there's plenty of green grass on the island and perfect breeding conditions. One sheep can produce several lambs at a go and let's assume that they all make it to adulthood because of those perfect conditions. So if each sheep is producing on average four lambs every year, then you would basically need 7000 divided by four sheep on the island, which equals approximately 1700 sheep to give birth and not be eaten.

So you'd need 7000 sheep in the first year, who would all get eaten. And you'd need another 1700 sheep to produce the next year's lot of sheep. So you would need approximately 8700 sheep to begin with.

Now, the assumptions made above may be a bit flaky and there is actually a precise mathematical formula you can apply to questions about perpetuities. But the interviewers are not looking for mathematical formulae – they're looking for the ability to make assumptions and apply rough rules.

If you are unsure about your ability to work through analytical problems, then practise them with a friend or ideally another job seeker. Take it in turns to devise simple questions such as the ones in this section to quiz each other.

I'd like you to multiply 8 by 9 and then take 13 away from the result

This question is a straightforward numerical challenge. Unlike the previous 'guesstimate' questions in this section, a right answer exists. 8 multiplied by 9 is, of course, 72. Taking 13 away from 72 gives you 59. But the challenge is whether you can do that calculation in your head – and quickly.

If applying for a job that involves numbers – anything from working as an analyst to working behind a bar or in a shop – practising your multiplication tables and mental arithmetic helps.

To prepare for such an interview, have a go at calculating the answers to the following sums – without using a calculator or even pen and paper of course!

- *What is 12 plus 36 plus 17?*

- *A pint of beer costs £1.23 in my bar. How much will a round of four pints cost?*

- *As quickly as possible, what is 6 times 8?*

- *I am expecting 60 guests in my restaurant tonight. Assuming that each person eats one-fifth of a cake, how many cakes will I need to buy?*

- *A customer buys some goods in our shop costing £11.16. She gives you a £50 note. How much change will you give her back?*

- *A customer says that your colleague has short-changed him. He was expecting 64p back but actually received 37p. How much would you need to give him back?*

You get the idea. If you don't feel comfortable doing these sums, make up some of your own and practise doing them in your head.

Don't worry if your times tables and mental arithmetic are a bit rusty at first. Practising daily soon gets you up to speed at this skill again.

Chapter 13

Coping with Illegal and Personal Questions

*I*nterviewers sometimes ask certain questions that make candidates feel uncomfortable. But in some cases you may feel uncomfortable not because these questions are terribly probing but because they enquire about your personal background, health, and life outside of work.

Many personal questions are actually illegal. Unfortunately, interviewers continue to ask them. In this chapter, I cover how to deal with such questions should they arise.

Countering Illegal Questions

Britain's employment legislation states that interviewers should not ask questions about age, marital status, children, religion, or nationality. However, though interviewers do sometimes ask these questions, they rarely do so knowingly breaking the law. The truth is that most interviewers have never had proper training and simply don't know that these questions are illegal.

You may be well within your rights to refuse to answer the questions in this section. Unfortunately, saying, *I refuse to answer that question because it is illegal*, is unlikely to get you the job. You may embarrass the interviewers, or they may simply decide to reject you because they find you difficult and obstructive!

In practice, proving that interviewers rejected you because they discriminated against you is very difficult. Would you rather take an employer to court to try to prove discrimination or would you rather try to get the job? You must decide for yourself how to deal with these questions. You can refuse to answer the question because it is illegal and discriminates against you. Or you can answer the question and try to impress the interviewers so much that the answer to the illegal question never becomes an issue. The choice is yours. If you want to brush up on your rights, check out Liz Barclay's *Small Business Employment Law For Dummies* (Wiley).

How old are you?

In practice, interviewers rarely ask this question because they can usually estimate your age from the number of years of experience that you have on your CV. Or they can guess your age from the date that you completed your GCSEs or graduated from university.

The government is introducing legislation to prohibit age discrimination as of October 2006. Technically, interviewers should consider candidates for any job irrespective of whether they are 19 or 59 years of age.

If the interviewers do ask this question, you need to decide for yourself how to answer it. Take a look at the following for inspiration:

✔ *I'm in my mid-forties and I have had nearly twenty years of experience in this field. I've spent the last three years working at a supervisory level – coaching and developing the team, scheduling work loads and rotas, and dealing with customer problems that get referred to me.*

✔ *I'd like to believe that age isn't an issue. I have the guts and determination to make it in this field. I've worked in this*

> *industry for nearly twenty years and have a track record of exceeding targets in six out of the last seven years. But if you would still like to know my age, I'm 53.*

> ✔ *I'm 39.*

The following are not technically illegal questions. But you should still have an answer for them if you think you're likely to be considerably older or younger than the other candidates for the job:

> ✔ *I have to admit that you're a lot older than the other candidates we're seeing. How do you think you'd cope with the job?*

> ✔ *If we were to offer you the position, how would you feel about being managed by someone a lot younger than you?*

> ✔ *We were ideally looking for a more mature candidate – why do you think you could do the job?*

If interviewers do comment on your relative age (either older or younger than they were looking for), avoid pointing out the illegality of their line of questioning – doing so can be seen as quite an aggressive approach! Instead, choose to refute their assertion that age is an issue by focusing on what you do bring to the party.

> ✔ *I understand that you might have had an older candidate in mind. For example, I'm the youngest branch manager in my area of 18 branches – but my branch was rated third highest in the area in terms of sales performance for the last year. So I have as much credibility with my team and experience in managing a branch as many managers much older than myself.*

> ✔ *Yes I might be older than you had been looking for. But I have a lot to bring that the younger candidates simply don't have. I have a lot of life experience and experience of dealing with customers of all age groups. And I know there's a perception that older people are stubborn or unwilling to learn, but I can assure you that I'm genuinely hungry for this kind of opportunity and would relish the chance to take on this role.*

Coping with age discrimination

Age discrimination comes in many forms, and obviously tends to affect older candidates – with employers assuming that older people are less motivated, committed, or take longer to learn the ropes. But age discrimination can also affect younger candidates too – with interviewers believing that younger candidates are more interested in partying and having fun than taking on responsibility.

Are you married?

This question really should not be asked, and sometimes engenders double standards in the interviewer's mind. Interviewers sometimes see marriage as a desirable quality in men – they may think that a man can be more successful with a doting wife at home. On the other hand, interviewers worry that a married woman may decide to have babies and then need to take maternity leave. This mindset is obviously discrimination on the part of interviewers, and you can use one of the following strategies against it:

- *I'm not married, but in any case what I hope to convince you of is the fact that I have a solid background in this area. I've been working as a technician now for six years and have experience of working with a wide range of equipment that I believe will be directly relevant to the position that you are recruiting for.*

- *I am married, but I am a big believer in separating my work life from my home life. I enjoy my job and am completely committed to developing in my career and working towards becoming a general manager within the next three to five years.*

- *I hope you won't take this the wrong way, but I'm afraid I don't see the relevance of the question to the job.*

Do you have children?

If the interviewers are asking you this question, they are probably worried that sudden illnesses amongst your kids or childcare issues may require you to take time off from work.

Rather than antagonise the interviewers by refusing to answer the question, your best bet is talking about the ironclad childcare arrangements you have in place.

See if you can craft a response based on one of the following:

✔ *Yes, we have two children. But we have a full-time nanny, so my working hours will never be an issue. In fact, I insisted on employing a full-time live-in nanny so that I could concentrate on my career.*

✔ *Yes, we have one girl, who is at school. But my parents live very nearby, so on the off chance that my partner is unable to look after Sarah, my parents are always happy to step into the breach.*

What are your childcare arrangements?

This is merely a variation on the question *Do you have children?* Reassure the interviewers that your childcare provision is able to cope with any demands that the job may place on you (see the preceding question for examples).

When do you plan to have children?

This is a poor question because it tends to be asked only of women and therefore discriminates unfairly against them. Some interviewers do not recognise that having children and having a career are not completely incompatible!

Your first response may be to say *It's none of your business* and you would have every right to be indignant. But that sort of answer isn't going to get you the job.

Be careful not to allow any irritation or aggression to creep into your voice when answering this question:

✔ *I have no plans to have children at the moment.*

✔ *I have certain career goals that I want to achieve first. I intend to finish my professional examinations in the next*

> *18 months and then hopefully become a manager. So I can't see that my partner and I would want to start a family for at least four or five years.*

Are you pregnant at the moment?

As a job interview should only be about ascertaining who is the best person for the job, asking this question discriminates unfairly against women (so is illegal to ask).

Although you would be perfectly within your rights to refuse to answer the question, your answer depends on how pregnant you look when you arrive at the interview! Also, bear in mind that if you refuse to answer the question and then end up taking six months off after having only worked at a company for a few months, you can be doing your future career prospects a real disservice.

Your best bet is to refuse to answer the question on the grounds that it is discriminatory. Here's one way to respond:

I'm surprised that you ask that question. Please don't take offence but I'd rather not answer questions about my personal life as I don't see their relevance to this job.

 When you actually get offered the job, admit that you are pregnant and see whether you can negotiate how and when to take maternity leave to suit the organisation as well as yourself.

Does your partner mind you being away from home?

Technically, this isn't an illegal question. If you have already mentioned that you have a partner, the interviewers may simply be concerned about the prospects of your having to travel extensively for your work.

 You can say that your partner's attitude to your work is none of the interviewers' business. But a less belligerent response stands you in better stead.

The interviewers may be less inclined to give you the job if they believe that time away from home may cause strife in your family life. Reassure them that this is not the case:

✔ *It's never been an issue. I believe that it is very important to visit all of the different branches in my patch at least once a month, which necessitates my being away from home three or even four nights a week. But that's simply the commitment I'm willing to make to this job.*

✔ *No, he doesn't mind. Having worked on these sorts of transactions for the last five years, he is very used to the fact that I may need to be with our European partners for up to several weeks at a time. But we both recognise that travelling is an integral and exciting part of my job.*

What is your sexual orientation?

This is clearly an illegal question: Your sexuality has nothing to do with your ability to do the job.

Asking this question is still illegal even if applying for a job at a faith school or a religious charity. Equally, a gay charity cannot refuse to employ you simply because you are straight. The only exception is if you are applying to become a priest or an imam.

Take a look at these two example responses to build your own answer from:

✔ *I'm sorry, but I'm not sure that I see why you're asking the question. Please don't read anything into this, but I'd rather not answer that question – simply because I don't quite see why it's relevant to the job.*

✔ *I have friends who are gay and straight and I feel comfortable working with both gay men and lesbians, but I am not gay myself. I hope that the fact that I am straight will not affect your judgement in choosing the strongest candidate for the job.*

What are your religious beliefs?

What on earth do the interviewers think is the relevance of your religion to the job? You may understand why the interviewer is asking the question – their ignorance about your religion may cause them to wonder whether you would be able to take on all aspects of the job.

Don't forget that interviewers rarely ask illegal questions because they want to deliberately flout the law. More often than not, they are simply ignorant of the law. So avoid letting your anger or annoyance show that the interviewers have asked such an impolite question.

Consider these example responses:

> ✔ *If you don't mind my honesty, I'm not sure I can see the relevance of that question to determining my suitability for the job. I've done a lot of research on the nature of the job and I am certain that my religion will never compromise my ability to do it. Having said that, I have no problem with telling you that I am a Sikh.*

> ✔ *Like a lot of people, I do have certain beliefs that guide how I behave in life. And one of my beliefs is to treat all people with respect at all times, which translates into a benefit for the colleagues and clients that I work for.*

> ✔ *I hope you won't take this the wrong way, but I'd prefer not to answer that question. I'd rather just say that I've read the job description carefully and read up on your company, too. And I can't see any reason why my beliefs would stop me from being a valued contributor in your organisation.*

Interviewers may ask if you need to take more holiday than other team members because they're ignorant of the ins and outs of the practices associated with your religion. Reassure the interviewers that you will not require more days off than other employees. If you need to take certain days off for religious reasons, say that you will do so only as part of your annual allowance of leave.

There are certain days that I would very much like to take off during the year. But I shall be putting in a request to take those as part of my annual leave in much the same way as any other employee.

Is English your mother tongue?

Employers are not allowed to discriminate against people because of their nationality. If your English is good enough for the job, then the law says that it should not matter whether you were taught it from birth as your native language or learnt it much later in life as a second, third, or even tenth language.

As it happens, English isn't my mother tongue. But as I hope I have been able to demonstrate in this interview, I am more than capable of dealing with both colleagues and customers in English.

A variation on the issue of language goes along the lines of: *I'm sorry, we're really looking for a French candidate rather than someone who speaks French.* This statement borders on outright discrimination. Employers are only allowed to reject candidates because of their job skill or lack of it – and not because of their nationality. So an employer can say that your grasp of French is not strong enough, but not that you aren't suitable because you are not French. Try to change the interviewers' minds without having to threaten taking them to court for their illegal views:

I'm very disappointed that you feel that way. Yes, I may not have been born a French national, but I completed my secondary education in France and have been working in France for seven years. Not only do I have a French accent that is indistinguishable from that of the local Parisians, but I have a very strong understanding of how business is conducted over there as well. To add to that, I also have a very good understanding of the particular market that you want the successful candidate to deal with.

Where were you born?

Your birthplace is irrelevant to your ability to do the job – so this is yet another illegal question. In deciding how to cope with this question, you must decide on a response that you ultimately feel comfortable with:

> ✔ *I was born in Frankfurt, in Germany. But I've lived in the UK since I was six, so I actually feel more British than German.*

> ✔ *I have dual nationality, so getting a work permit wouldn't be an issue.*
>
> ✔ *I was born in Canada, but I've lived here for three years now and have British citizenship.*

Of course, you must have the relevant citizenship or work permits to allow you to work in the country. Unless applying for a very important and senior role, most companies automatically reject you if you don't have clearance, as the application process is usually more hassle than a new employee is worth. If you do have the right work permits, you won't need to bring them along with you to interview. But be prepared to show them to the HR department or other relevant persons if the interviewers ultimately offer you the job.

Have you ever been arrested?

This is a tricky question. Being arrested should have no bearing on your ability to do the job, but lying about an arrest can still get you in hot water. Yes, if you have ever been convicted of any offences, then you need to disclose them. But if you have been arrested but released without charge, then the government says that you are a free person. Remember the adage 'Innocent until proven guilty'. The best answer to this question is *No*. But if you have been arrested, you may want to fudge your answer a little:

I'd like to assure you that I have no criminal convictions that you should be worried about!

You can also legitimately say no if your conviction has been spent – meaning a relevant time period has elapsed since your offence. Consult the National Association for the Care and Resettlement of Offenders telephone helpline on 0800 0181 259 or their Web site www.nacro.org.uk for more information on spent convictions.

Dealing with discrimination

You need to decide on your own tactic for handling discriminatory questions. After all, just because an interviewer asks the question does not mean that they will necessarily be prejudiced against you for being older or younger, a woman or man, having children, being gay, or being of a particular religious denomination or nationality.

However, if you do feel that you have been rejected because of discrimination, then your first port of call may be to contact your local Citizens Advice Bureau (CAB). You can find out the contact details of your nearest CAB on the Web site: www. citizensadvice.org.uk.

The Advisory, Conciliation and Arbitration Service (ACAS) also has an informative website: www.acas. org.uk.

Alternatively, you can try talking to someone on the TUC's Know Your Rights advice hotline: 0870 600 4882 (national rate, advisors available from 8 a.m. to 10 p.m.).

Both of these sources can advise you on whether taking further action is appropriate, and how to proceed with it.

Talking about Life Outside of Work

Many interviewers feel that asking you about your interests outside of work tells them a lot about the kind of person you are. Are you the sort of person to fit into their team?

Interestingly enough, employment legislation says that interviewers cannot ask questions about how you spend your time outside of work. In the eyes of the law, whether you spend five hours every evening watching television or engaging in team sports and helping disabled children technically has no bearing on your ability to do your day job. You, therefore, need to decide whether you are willing to possibly jeopardise your chances of getting the job by stating your rights and refusing to answer these questions.

What do you do with your leisure time?

Some interviewers believe that candidates who achieve in their life outside of work are more likely to achieve at work. Interviewers ask this question most frequently of candidates in their twenties and early thirties who may not have a lot of work experience behind them.

Employers are impressed by group activities. Employers also like candidates who engage in sporting pursuits. Engaging in competitive team sports wins you the most brownie points.

Can you come up with a response like one of these?

✔ *I play in a Sunday rugby league. It's more friendly than intensely competitive, but I do train at least once a week with the team and try to spend some time jogging and keeping fit for matches too.*

✔ *I was a keen netball player at university and represented my department in intramural competitions. Since graduating and moving down to London, I've not yet had the time to find a local group that I can play with – but it's at the top of my agenda once I've found a job.*

✔ *I'm chair of a local neighbourhood regeneration group. There's a lot of graffiti in the area and we get together to remove it. I chair meetings once every month or so and also participate in the clean-up activities.*

Your leisure interests seem very solitary – does this affect your team skills?

Perhaps you enjoy going to the gym or swimming; perhaps you play a musical instrument at home or enjoy painting or exercising your artistic talents. In any case, the interviewers may be worried that you're a bit of an introvert and perhaps unsuited to a busy, social workplace such as theirs? Put them right with an answer along these lines:

I've never really thought about my hobby that way. I guess playing the piano could be seen as solitary. But to be honest, in my current job I have a team of thirteen people. And at home I have three children. So playing my piano is a way for me to spend just half an hour a day on my own. But it doesn't mean that I don't like people!

What sports do you play?

Interviewers who ask this question probably play sports themselves and believe that sports players may have certain skills or traits that non-sports players don't have. If you play any sports, mention them (see 'What do you do with your leisure time?' earlier in this chapter). If you don't, try to deflect the question. Try one of the following:

✔ *I don't play any sports because I find that my working pattern means that I can't commit to doing anything with a team. But I do go to the gym a couple of times a week.*

✔ *I used to play tennis. But I suffered an injury a couple of years ago and have been unable to do any vigorous activity. However, I try to walk as much as I can to stay fit and there's still nothing I enjoy more than watching a live tennis match!*

✔ *I don't play any sports, but I do keep busy outside of work. In addition, I walk for around half an hour each day – both to and from work – so that keeps me fit.*

Do you read much?

The interviewers may be trying to understand whether you're the kind of person who is interested in furthering your knowledge and bettering yourself.

Despite the fact that this is a closed question, don't just answer *Yes*. Go on to give some examples of what you enjoy reading and why.

I try to read as much as having a busy job and a family allows. My favourite genre is twentieth-century autobiographies – I find it absolutely fascinating to find out more about figures in the public eye.

However, you can get away with saying that you do not read much if you have other team- or group-based activities (such as participating in community events or team sports) to talk about.

To be honest, between my job, the local football league, and the Make A Wish foundation, I don't have that much time to read. But when I was on holiday over the summer, I did get through a couple of books.

What was the last book you read?

This isn't a trick question. Just make sure that you don't lie in an attempt to appear clever. Yes, it may impress the interviewers if you tell them that you read a cutting-edge management book. But will you be able to go on to talk about it in depth if the interviewers have read it too? Here are a couple of responses:

✔ *The last book I read was on marketing strategy by a professor at Harvard Business School. It was a bit over-long, but it had some good ideas about how to segment and target customers.*

✔ *I just got back from holiday a couple of weeks ago. So I was reading a thriller that I picked up at the airport. It was pure escapist fun.*

Have an example ready in your head so that you don't have to admit that you can't remember the author or the exact name of the title!

What was the last film you saw?

The interviewer may just be making conversation with you in an attempt to help you relax. On the other hand, the interviewer may be a bit of an amateur psychologist and be trying to analyse your personality based on your taste in films.

Don't stop at just telling the interviewers the name of the last film you saw. Go on to explain what you thought of it or why you enjoyed it.

> ✔ *It was* The Diary of Loneliness *by the Spanish director
> Pedro Almodóvar. It has excellent cinematography – some
> beautiful scenery shots. And it was an interesting film about
> how people's relationships evolve as they get older.*

> ✔ *I think the last film I saw was the* Fantastic Five. *I took my
> children to see it and I have to say that the jokes are writ-
> ten on two levels – both for children and adults. I quite
> enjoyed it actually.*

Do you keep up with current affairs?

The only good answer is to say, *Yes*, that you read a newspaper at least every weekday. If you say *No*, you may as well con-
fess to having no idea of what is going on in the world around
you. Unfortunately, interviewers also take a dim view of candidates who claim to keep up with current affairs by watching
the news on TV!

Don't lie if you don't read a paper. A better strategy is to pick
up a quality newspaper every day for at least two to three
weeks before a big interview in order to brush up on current
affairs. Think of reading a newspaper as a vital part of invest-
ing in your chances of securing a great job.

You can get bonus points for mentioning any notable radio
shows that you listen to on a regular basis – for example, any
programmes covering politics, business, the arts, or other
current affairs topics.

What newspaper do you read?

This is often a follow-up question to 'Do you keep up with
current affairs?' (covered previously). It may seem like a
straightforward enough question. But tread carefully as
there are multiple traps laying in wait for you!

A major trap concerns sending out messages about your class
and political leanings. For example, *The Guardian* is often seen
as being positioned as left of centre, while *The Telegraph* is
sometimes viewed as being quite right wing. Why not balance
this out by reading a perceived left-wing paper during the
week, and taking a perceived right-wing one at the weekend?

Some interviewers are also quite snooty about preferring candidates who read broadsheets rather than tabloids or even mid-market newspapers such as *The Daily Mail*.

What news story has grabbed your attention recently?

This question is the ultimate test of whether you have been reading and absorbing news items or not. Unfortunately, I can't supply you with an answer – you really need to have read the newspapers and other relevant publications in your field to be able to construct an appropriate answer.

If any notable trade publications cover your particular industry, brush up on these before a big interview. For example, financiers and City bankers regard *Financial News* as a vital read, while people in television follow the goings-on in *Broadcast*.

Talking About Your Health

Interviewers are loath to take on candidates who have had major medical problems for fear of employing someone who may need to take a lot of time off work or land them with costly medical bills. A lot of candidates choose not to mention their health on their CV or application form because they would prefer to explain it face-to-face to an interviewer rather than be rejected out of hand.

Questions about your health are not necessarily illegal – but that doesn't mean that they aren't nosy and often inappropriate! If questions about your health crop up at interview, you should ideally reassure the interviewers that you have now fully recovered. If you can't do that, then at least try to play down the problem – but remember never to lie!

Questions about your health shouldn't really come up in interviews, but if they do, this section helps you to understand the best way to give your answers.

You mention that you took a lot of time off last year – why is that?

Uh-oh! This is the question that you've been dreading. There's no way around the truth, but explain the problem as briefly as possible – avoid getting into messy medical detail if you can – and then try to move off the topic.

Practise your answer to this question and think carefully about the precise words and phrases that you use. Avoid letting slip phrases such as . . . *I'm now back to work but I still feel some pain occasionally* and just tell the interviewers *I'm now back to work.*

You can try to divert the interviewers' attention by focusing on your strengths and the many good reasons to employ you rather than letting them dwell on the one possible reason not to employ you.

Consider these two very different examples of reasons for time off work:

- ✔ *I had an accident at home – I slipped off a ladder and hurt my shoulder. Unfortunately, I had to take five weeks off work to recover. After that time away, though, I was really pleased to be able to get back to work. Thankfully, with the help of a good physiotherapist, I've now recovered.*

- ✔ *I had a minor heart attack two years ago. In retrospect, I was probably a walking time bomb as I used to smoke and was quite overweight. But the heart attack was a real wake-up call. Since then I have given up smoking, changed my diet, and lost about two stone. In a strange way, I actually feel fitter and more able to do my job now than I did ten years ago!*

How many days did you take off sick last year?

This is a purely factual question. If you cannot recall the precise number of days that you had off sick, then at least try to estimate the number.

I had around seven weeks off work. But I'd like to reiterate that I've now recovered fully from that problem.

Don't lie about the number of days you had to take off work! This is the kind of fact that employers frequently check – and a lie in the interview can easily let you down later on.

Do you have any medical conditions that you should tell us about?

If you do, answer this question in a succinct fashion. Try to get across that you are otherwise in good health and ready to launch yourself into a new job.

You're not required to tell the interviewers about past illnesses nor feel obligated to predict what the future may bring either. However, if you are comfortable answering questions about your health, here are some examples.

> ✔ *I can assure you that I'm fully able to take on the demands of this job. I've had diabetes for nearly ten years now, and it has never interfered with my ability to do the job. In fact, I'd put money on the fact that you would find me a more hard-working and committed person than most of the other candidates you'll find out there.*

> ✔ *I do have a condition called Raynaud's phenomenon, which basically means that I occasionally feel discomfort in my fingers. But in consultation with my doctor, I'm in control of the condition. It hasn't stopped me from doing a very good job and, as I mentioned earlier, I did win the Employee of the Month award back in June.*

Choose your words carefully. For example, if you have ongoing symptoms, try replacing the word 'pain' with 'discomfort'. Too much detail can unfortunately cost you the job!

How do you cope with your disability?

This is a very bad question. Employers are only supposed to discuss the topic of disabilities *after* they have offered the job to the strongest candidate (hopefully you!). Again, however, interviewers may not realise that they've fallen foul of the law. So the best strategy is to assure the interviewers that your disability isn't a problem rather than being testy and reminding them of the law.

> ✔ *I have been in a wheelchair for the last six years and I don't consider myself to be disabled. I lead a very active life and pride myself on the fact that I am entirely self-sufficient and I continue to be a strong contributor to the teams that I have been a part of.*

> ✔ *I walk with a stick, which means that I am totally self-sufficient when it comes to making my way to and from work, as well as around the workplace. I do require the use of a larger computer screen and some specialised software. But there are government grants for these, so this wouldn't have any cost implications for you at all. In summary, you could treat me pretty much as any other employee. In fact, I would expect to be treated exactly the same as any other worker.*

Chapter 14

Taking Control in Unusual Situations

. . . .

In This Chapter

▶ Finessing panel interviews

▶ Handling informal interviews

▶ Dealing with technology

▶ Squaring up to psychometric tests

▶ Succeeding at assessment centres

. . . .

*T*he traditional interview involves one or two interviewers and you, perhaps across a desk or a table in an office. However, all sorts of other types of interview can be offered to you. In this chapter, I cover some of the other situations and devious challenges that interviewers can use to test and evaluate candidates.

Dealing with Panel Interviews

In a panel interview, you may find yourself confronted with a row of up to eight or ten interviewers. Panel interviews are particularly popular in the public sector and for more senior roles.

To pass panel interviews with flying colours, follow these tips:

> ✔ Follow the lead of the interviewers. If faced with many interviewers, you may not be offered the chance to shake hands and say hello to each of them. In some cases, not all the interviewers even introduce themselves.

✔ Maintain eye contact mainly with the person on the panel who asks you each question. Do look occasionally at the other panel members when answering the question, but for the most part maintain eye contact with the person who actually asked you it.

✔ Don't let yourself be put off by a panel. The questions fly at you from all corners, but take your time to answer each at your own pace.

✔ Prepare for panel interview questions as you would any other type of interview.

Never assume that any of the panel members are unimportant. A common ruse used by interviewers is to pretend that one of them is merely a note taker.

Handling Hi-Tech Interviews

Employers know that technology can drastically reduce the costs of recruitment. Especially when you or the interviewers are busy, they may want to conduct an initial interview by telephone or via video conferencing. The interviewers may then invite a shortlist of candidates to a second round, face-to-face interview.

Hanging on the telephone

Telephone interviews are tricky because establishing rapport or conveying your enthusiasm for the job without the face-to-face element of most interviews is difficult. However, you can create a positive impression on the phone if you always:

✔ Eliminate background noises.

✔ Smile when speaking.

✔ Use verbal cues (such as *I see* and *That's interesting*) instead of nodding and eye contact.

✔ Have copies of your CV or application form in front of you.

✔ Thank the interviewer at the end.

Make sure you get the interviewer's name and contact details and consider sending a thank you e-mail or letter afterwards to maximise your chances of getting the job (see Chapter 16).

Handling video conferencing and Webcams with finesse

Video conferencing tends to be restricted to high-level appointments, but a growing number of employers are exploiting Webcam technology to conduct first interviews over the Internet.

Follow this advice to help your hi-tech interview run smoothly:

- ✔ Dress smartly.
- ✔ Avoid wearing too much white (beware screen glare!).
- ✔ Check your Webcam settings.
- ✔ Speak more slowly than normal (watch out for time lags).
- ✔ Avoid using hand gestures (they blur on screen).

If you experience any technical problems – such as not being able to see or hear the interviewers clearly – speak up immediately! Don't expect the problem to go away of its own accord.

Getting Ready for Psychometric Tests

Two broad categories of psychometric test exist. *Aptitude tests* have right and wrong answers – these most commonly measure skills such as numeracy, verbal reasoning, and spatial awareness. *Personality tests* measure your preferences in certain situations and you don't have to worry about 'right' or 'wrong' answers, because they don't exist.

Passing aptitude tests

Aptitude tests are daunting if you haven't done them before. When you're invited to an interview, find out if you must complete one of these tests.

By far the commonest aptitude tests measure verbal reasoning and numeracy skills. Some employers may also devise their own tests for spatial reasoning – for example, if you're applying for a job as an engineer.

Almost all aptitude tests are timed. Read the instructions carefully to see how much time you have for the entire test. If you find you're struggling with a single question for more than a couple of minutes, move on to the next question to avoid dropping too many points.

Every time you encounter a different aptitude test, read the instructions carefully. Precisely how much time do you have for the questionnaire? And exactly how should you respond? For example, some tests ask you to circle the correct response; others ask you to underline the correct response or fill in a small circle. A few tests ask you to select more than one answer per question. *Never* make any assumptions about the instructions – read them carefully.

Completing personality questionnaires

Personality tests assess how you typically respond to different situations. Would you rate yourself as a tough or fairly sensitive person? Would you say that you tend to be very talkative or a bit quiet at work?

Personality tests are not usually timed. But the best way to complete them is to read through the questions and jot down your response fairly quickly. The more you mull over the responses, the more likely you are to confuse yourself.

Be careful not to try to second-guess the aim behind the personality test. Many candidates think that they should answer as if they are more extroverted and outgoing than they actually are. But sometimes an employer may be looking to reject candidates who are *too* extroverted in case they get bored of the job quickly.

Succeeding at Assessment Centres

Organisations that use competency-based interviews (see Chapter 9) often invite candidates to *assessment centres*. At these events, the people scrutinising you are often called *assessors* rather than interviewers. The assessors don't simply ask candidates to talk about their skills – they want to observe those skills in action.

 That an assessment centre is a real place – such as a specially designed building for putting candidates through their paces – is a common misconception. But the term actually means a collection of different techniques for scrutinising how candidates perform in different situations. Assessment centres can be held at a variety of locations, from the organisation's own offices to a hotel or conference centre.

Passing in-trays

In-tray tests are designed to simulate a day in the office and to test your ability to assimilate and prioritise information.

An in-tray usually consists of a collection of paperwork such as letters, reports, and printouts. Usually, some of the items are very important while many others may have been put in to distract you. They may be based on an entirely fictitious business or they may be made-up items concerning a real business.

Some modern organisations may even simulate a real day in the office by providing you with a computer and a telephone. You may have to type up a report or send e-mails to colleagues and customers while taking phone calls – the whole experience can be quite tough if you're not ready for it!

 Read the instructions carefully and identify the key points. Too many candidates go wrong simply by misreading what they're supposed to do.

Follow these tips to do well at in-trays:

- ✔ **Look for themes:** Always begin by skim-reading all the items to get a sense of any overarching topics that may link individual items.

- ✔ **Identify key issues:** Prioritise the crucial items that need handling.

- ✔ **Prioritise your actions:** Develop a rough idea in your head as to a ranking for issues within the in-tray. Tackle the ones at the top of your list first.

- ✔ **Differentiate between action and further investigation:** Although you may be expected to take action on certain urgent and critical issues, the assessors may be looking for good candidates to notice that certain issues require further investigation before a course of action can be decided upon.

Look for guidelines within the in-tray documents as to the team or organisation's priorities. These guidelines are typically written by your line manager or a more senior manager (such as the managing director, chairperson, or CEO). These guidelines can be labelled *key initiatives*, *vision/value statements*, *company imperatives*, and so on. Show the assessors that you take into account organisational rules by ensuring that all your proposed actions align with these guidelines.

Giving great presentations

You may be asked by the assessors to give a presentation so they can examine your oral communication skills. Employers are increasingly looking for people who can not only convey factual information clearly, but also do it in an engaging and interesting way.

The assessors are evaluating not only *what* you say but also *how* you say it. Make sure that you maintain good eye contact with the assessors and use inflection in your voice to make the presentation come to life (see Chapter 3 for more on developing these skills).

Some employers ask candidates to prepare a presentation beforehand; others may give candidates a topic during the assessment centre and set aside time for them to prepare a presentation.

Here are some pointers for giving a great presentation:

- ✔ Watch the clock.
- ✔ Create a structure for your presentation.
- ✔ Focus on a small number of key points.
- ✔ Use simple visual aids.
- ✔ Prepare for questions.

The key to giving presentations is *don't overcomplicate*. Covering a small number of crucial points is better than exhaustively wittering on about a topic.

Excelling at group exercises

The assessors may gather a group of candidates – usually some number between three and eight people – together and ask you all to discuss a topic or engage in a task while they observe you. The key in these exercises is to demonstrate that you're confident, but not arrogant, and that you can be a team player without dominating the discussion or being rude.

Group exercises can vary enormously, but some popular ones include:

- ✔ Discussing a topic in the news.
- ✔ Constructing a tower out of children's play bricks.
- ✔ Evaluating a business idea and coming up with recommendations for taking it further.

Be sure to read the instructions carefully, picking up on the precise nature of the task or topic of conversation.

Here are some tips for handling group exercises:

- ✔ Encourage others to speak.
- ✔ Watch your body language.
- ✔ Build on others' suggestions.
- ✔ Demonstrate your enthusiasm.

Being a star in role play simulations

The assessors may ask you to role play a scenario similar to the job you're applying for. For example, if applying for a managerial position, they may ask you to discipline an actor pretending to be an unruly member of your team.

Bear in mind that the organisation has probably invested a lot of time and money in designing the simulation and training managers or even bringing in consultants to run it. So make sure that you behave as if the situation was serious. If you say that you 'don't like role plays' or don't play along, expect to be marked down automatically.

The key in role plays is to think about the nature of the job that you're applying for. Decide upon the required skills and try to demonstrate them throughout. For example, if you're applying for a customer service job that requires tact and diplomacy, make sure that you behave tactfully and diplomatically when talking to other candidates in a group exercise.

Role play simulations test not only what you say but also how you say it. Make sure that your body language is consistent with what you are talking about – for example, demonstrating empathy or enthusiasm in your facial expressions, tone of voice, and use of hands.

Role play simulations vary enormously from job to job and organisation to organisation. However, here are some common tasks:

 ✔ Meeting an angry customer.

 ✔ Selling products or services to a new client.

 ✔ Disciplining a member of your team.

Be yourself. Candidates often go wrong when they attempt to second-guess what the assessors are looking for. Just behave as if you were actually facing these situations. Don't try to be someone that you're not.

Part IV
Securing the Job of Your Dreams

"Well, Mr Pitherington, congratulations, I think you'll fit in very well into our organisation."

In this part . . .

The secret to getting a job does not rely solely on answering tough interview questions well. At some point, the interviewers turn the tables and offer you the opportunity to ask them some questions. And asking the right kinds of questions can make a big difference in how the interviewers see you.

In this part, I take you through how to research the company and ask questions to impress the interviewers with your brilliance. I also focus on how to finish interviews with a flourish and follow up with interviewers to best effect. And, if you're unlucky enough not to get the job, I tell you how to make sure that you benefit from your mistakes and improve after every interview you go to. But let's not dwell on what may happen, let's try to nail every single interview!

Chapter 15

Asking Great Questions

....

In This Chapter

▶ Demonstrating how much you want the job

▶ Ascertaining your future career prospects

▶ Asking about the organisation's culture

▶ Developing your formal questions into an informal discussion

....

As the interview draws to a close, the interviewers will almost certainly ask you: *Do you have any questions for us?*

Interviewers often judge candidates on the nature of the questions that you ask. For example, asking about the hours and the number of annual leave days you're entitled to can give them the impression that you are a bit of a slacker, interested only in how little work you can get away with. Or asking about the pay and benefits can make you sound greedy.

In this chapter, I cover how to research great questions that not only impress the interviewers but also help you to decide whether this is an organisation that you would actually want to work for.

Never ever say that you have no questions. Saying that you have nothing to ask is a very poor response and signals to the interviewers that you aren't really that interested in the job.

Preparing the Right Questions for the Right Interview

You really do need to do some research to prepare a good dozen or more questions for the interviewers. This way, even if the interviewers tell you a lot about the job and their company, you're still able to ask a few questions at the end of the interview.

When asked if you have any questions, you may be tempted to say, *No, because we've already covered all of my questions in the discussion so far.* The problem is that – even if you are telling the truth – the interviewers may just decide that you simply had not prepared any questions.

Stuck for questions to ask?

If applying for a managerial role, consider asking questions such as:

- ✔ What are the members of the team like?

- ✔ Does the team have any issues that need sorting out? Are there any people who are underutilised?

- ✔ Who are the key decision makers in the organisation?

- ✔ What sort of budget would I have for running the team?

- ✔ What do you see as the main challenges facing the team at the moment?

- ✔ What style of management is the team used to?

- ✔ Are there any major milestones or deliverables that you expect the successful candidate to achieve?

- ✔ What kind of development programmes do you have for managers?

If interviewed for a part-time or job share position, you may want to ask questions such as:

- ✔ How do you see this position fitting in with the rest of the team?

- ✔ Do you have any other people in a similar position at the moment? How is the role working out for them?

- ✔ How would I be expected to hand over work to the other job share person and vice versa?

If the position is a short-term contract, ask a few of the following questions:

- ✔ Exactly how long is the contract?

- ✔ What are the deliverables within this time frame?

- ✔ When do you hope for this project to start?

- ✔ How likely is it that you may extend the contract or make it a full-time appointment?

- ✔ Assuming everything goes well, are there any realistic opportunities to join your organisation on a full-time basis?

 The number of questions you want to ask tends to depend on the seniority of the job. For entry level or junior management roles, aim to ask just three or four questions. For senior jobs, you may be expected to have plenty more questions – perhaps as many as ten or a dozen. If you struggle to think of questions when preparing for your interview, take inspiration from the sidebar 'Stuck for questions to ask?'

 Always check that a question is relevant to the particular role that you are applying for. For example, *Will I have a development budget?* is not a sensible question for entry-level or junior positions with no responsibilities in this area.

 Whatever job you go for, always aim to ask at least three or four questions about the job to demonstrate that you are genuinely interested in being taken on.

Tailoring your questions

Interviewers are most impressed by candidates who can actively demonstrate knowledge of their company. You can really stand out by asking questions that show you've done your research and want to delve even further into understanding the organisation. However, devising questions that are totally pertinent requires more effort on your part. The trick is to mention in passing the source of your knowledge before asking your question. Look at these examples for how to drop your sources into conversation:

✔ *I saw from your Web site that you sell mainly European wines. Do you have any plans to sell New World wines at all?*

✔ *Your brand is well known for its skincare products, and I've read rumours in the papers that you* are thinking about launching a fragrance range. Is there any truth in that?*

✔ *One of the press releases on your Web site says that you're planning to double your number of stores in the next five years. Realistically, what promotion prospects will this lead to for people like me?*

✔ *I read in the papers that you plan to close another dozen branches by the end of the year. How is that affecting the morale of the team?*

✔ *That you're seeking to grow the private equity side of the business has been widely publicised. What practical implications would that have for me if I were to join the business?*

When preparing questions to ask an employer, make sure that your questions can only be answered face-to-face by the interviewers. Asking a question easily answered by reading the job advert or their Web site won't help your prospects! Read the company's recruitment brochure (if it has one), job description, and any other documents that they make available to you. The sidebar 'Tailoring your questions' gives you even more advice.

Showing enthusiasm for the job

Here are some questions to ask showing that you are interested in the day-to-day nature of the job itself:

- ✔ *In this job, what would I be doing on a day-to-day basis?*
- ✔ *Do you have any idea of what proportion of my time would be spent on those tasks?*
- ✔ *What kind of training would I get initially?*
- ✔ *In practice, how much time would you expect me to spend seeing customers as opposed to being in the office?*
- ✔ *Who will be my line manager? What is it like to work for them?*
- ✔ *How much contact with customers am I likely to have initially?*
- ✔ *How will my performance be measured?*
- ✔ *What are the longer-term opportunities for working across the organisation?*
- ✔ *Will there be opportunities to work in any of your overseas offices?*

Never forget to prepare questions suitable for each specific interview that you go to. Never take the same questions along to different interviews as the interviewers are bound to see through you. For example, one job advert may be a bit vague about the daily nature of the job, while another may be very detailed – so asking about what you would be doing on a day-to-day basis in the second instance makes you sound poorly prepared.

You can also try to find out why the employer is looking to recruit someone at this time:

> ✔ *Why has this vacancy arisen?*
>
> ✔ *How many people are you looking to take on at this point in time?*
>
> ✔ *What happened to the previous holder of this position?* and (if that person was promoted) *Of course I'm interested in the next step up, so what did that person do to get that promotion?*
>
> ✔ *How quickly are you looking for someone to take on this role?*
>
> ✔ *How do you see this role developing?*

 Avoid asking questions about pay and benefits until you have been offered a job. In the early stages of the interviewing process, you make a far better impression by appearing interested in the job itself rather than focusing on how much you'll earn.

Checking out future prospects

Employers are usually keen to retain and develop staff rather than let them leave and then have to go through the bother of replacing them. So demonstrating that you're interested in working for the organisation for some years to come is always a good idea.

Here are some questions to ask about your own learning and development within the company:

> ✔ *What is your policy on staff development?*
>
> ✔ *Will I have a development budget?*
>
> ✔ *How do other people at this level tend to spend their development budget?*
>
> ✔ *Are there opportunities to change roles further down the line?*

You can also ask about possibilities for advancement and promotion in the future:

> ✔ *Does a formal appraisal system exist here?*
>
> ✔ *What criteria will be used to judge my suitability for promotion?*
>
> ✔ *How quickly do people in this role tend to be promoted? Is there a minimum length of time that you have to be in the role before you can be considered for promotion?*
>
> ✔ *Does the company encourage people to study for professional qualifications? If it does, what kind of support is the company willing to provide?*
>
> ✔ *What kinds of career paths do people take in the organisation?*

If you want to demonstrate that you take a 'bigger picture' interest in the nature of the organisation, try some of these questions on for size:

> ✔ *How does this department/division interface with others across the organisation?*
>
> ✔ *Are you able to talk about the company's plans for growth?*
>
> ✔ *What sorts of new products/services is the business planning to launch?*
>
> ✔ *Does the company have any plans for mergers or acquisitions?*
>
> ✔ *How stable is the business? Does the company ever have any cash flow problems?*
>
> ✔ *Has the company ever had to make any redundancies? Why? What happened?*
>
> ✔ *Is the organisation planning to restructure or undergo any change programmes in the near future?*

Enquiring about the culture

All organisations have rules and regulations. But *culture* describes the unwritten rules of how to behave at work. You can probably get an idea of the official rules or regulations by reading widely. But you can only get an idea of an organisation's culture by talking to people about it.

Questions about culture are very incisive. At worst, they can appear overly inquisitive so make sure to keep your tone light. And if you sense that the interviewers are prickling at your questions, move off the topic of culture immediately.

Here are some general questions to ask on the topic of organisational culture:

- ✔ *How would you describe the culture of the organisation?*
- ✔ *To what extent do people socialise together outside of work?*
- ✔ *How much autonomy do people really get in this organisation?*
- ✔ *What is it like to work here? What do you most enjoy about the job?*
- ✔ *Obviously you enjoy working here, but what would you say are your minor niggles or frustrations?*
- ✔ *How would you describe morale in the business at the moment?*
- ✔ *What does it take to be successful here?*
- ✔ *What kinds of people don't make it in this organisation?*

I can't stress this point enough – a fine line exists between asking intelligent questions and sounding like a show off! Be sure to think through the impact that each of your questions is likely to have on your interviewers. For example, if applying for a job as an entry-level role in customer service, asking about autonomy in the role would be far less appropriate than when applying for a supervisory role.

Turning Your Questions into a Discussion

When asking your questions, try to sound interested in the answers that the interviewers give. If the interviewers feel that you are genuinely interested in the position and their organisation, they're more likely to start thinking of you as a potential colleague rather than just another candidate.

Never ask a question purely for the sake of asking a question. You want your questions to leave the interviewers thinking that you have a genuine interest in joining their company. Don't rattle through a list of questions simply to demonstrate how clever you are.

As you ask your questions, try to find out more by making comments and asking further open-ended questions, such as:

- *That's interesting. How did that come about?*
- *May I ask more about that?*
- *So what does that mean for the organisation?*
- *That sounds intriguing – can you tell me more about that?*

Show your appreciation for the interviewers' patience in telling you more by commenting and nodding occasionally. If you fire too many questions at them, the interviewers can quickly feel that they are being interrogated – and that is not the effect you are trying to achieve!

Chapter 16

Dotting 'I's and Crossing 'T's

- -

In This Chapter

▶ Finishing an interview on a high note

▶ Writing follow-up letters to interviewers

▶ Gathering positive references

▶ Seeing the light and developing interview techniques further

- -

*I*n this chapter, I cover how to finish an interview with a flourish and also how to deal with next steps in the follow up to an interview.

Wrapping Up the Interview

When all the interview questions have been asked, and you've given your best answers and asked any questions you have about the job, you've got two last points to cover and then you're home free!

Checking the next steps

Sometimes an interviewer may already have explained the steps that follow an interview; the usual practice is to choose the right candidate and let the unsuccessful candidates know after their first choice accepts. However, if no one has done so, then you may want to ask about next steps. Simply ask: *And finally, what are the next steps?*

Handling spontaneous job offers

On rare occasions, the interviewers may be so bowled over by you that they decide to offer you the job on the spot. Perhaps you are the last candidate of the day or they are just totally amazed by you! Firstly, well done. But here are some pointers for dealing with such offers:

✔ **Convey your delight at the offer:** Tell the interviewers that you are very pleased and excited. Even if you're unsure about whether you want the job, act as if do – you can always turn it down later.

✔ **Play for time:** Explain that you are very excited but obviously would like to see a written offer and contract before accepting.

✔ **Avoid accepting the offer:** Even if you believe that this is your dream job, stop yourself from saying yes straightaway. If you accept the offer immediately, you may compromise your chances of negotiating a better deal for yourself.

Make sure that you understand whether there may be other stages to the interview process. Many employers, for example, may invite candidates in for several rounds of interviews. Or they may require candidates to complete a battery of psychometric tests or even attend an assessment centre (see Chapter 14 for more on these).

Never ask at the end of an interview whether you can call the interviewers for feedback should you be unsuccessful. You need to leave the interviewers with the impression that you're brimming with confidence that you'll be offered the job.

Making a great final impression

When the interviewers stand up, take that as a signal to leave. Although you may be tempted to just say goodbye and go, departure actually provides a critical opportunity for you to make one final pitch to the interviewers.

Everybody knows that first impressions count. Psychologists call that first impression the *primacy effect*. Interestingly enough though, research suggests that what you do or say in your last few minutes can also have a disproportionately large impact on the interviewers; this reaction is called the *recency effect* – meaning that the interviewers will remember your words and demeanour just before leaving.

Thank the interviewers and make a short statement to sell yourself. Either reiterate how interested and excited you are about the prospect of joining this company, or reinforce a couple of your key strengths. Say something along the lines of the following:

> ✔ *I've really enjoyed meeting you and having the chance to find out a bit more about the business. It sounds like there are some fascinating opportunities ahead!*

> ✔ *It sounds like a great opportunity – I'm sure it would be a very enjoyable challenge for me to take on. I look forward to hearing from you soon.*

> ✔ *Having had this discussion, I'd like to say that I'm extremely interested in the position. Although I'm looking at a couple of opportunities at the moment, I get the feeling that this one would suit me down to the ground.*

> ✔ *Thanks for making the time to meet with me. I hope that I've managed to convey the fact that I'm really excited about the possibility of working with you.*

Finally, shake hands with the interviewers – maintaining strong eye contact and smiling broadly all the time – and then leave.

Taking Notes after the Interview

After your interview, take some time to jot down what happened during it. Take a sheet of blank paper (or type up a word processing document or spreadsheet) and complete the following questions:

> ✔ What were the main questions they asked me?

> ✔ What questions did I ask the interviewers?

> ✔ What are the next steps? When should I contact them if I have not heard?

> ✔ What did I like about the company?

> ✔ What are my concerns about the company?

Try to write up your post-interview notes on the same day as the interview, while the events are still fresh in your mind. You'll be amazed at how quickly the details fade after even only a single night's sleep.

Now, you may be wondering why taking notes after an interview is necessary. But doing so has two benefits:

✔ Going through the process of writing down some of the key points about the interview and the interviewers helps you to decide whether you want to accept the job.

✔ Taking notes helps you to evaluate your own performance during the interview if you aren't successful.

Keep the notes you make, and refer to them when assessing how your interview went (see the section 'Evaluating the Experience', later in this chapter).

Sending Follow-Up Letters

Interviewers can take days to make up their minds. So you have an opportunity to influence interviewers even after you've left the interview.

If the interviewers are deliberating between you and perhaps one other candidate, then a follow-up letter can just tip the balance. A few well-crafted paragraphs can well be the difference between success and failure.

Consider carefully whether to use e-mail or an old-fashioned letter in an envelope with a stamp on it. E-mail can be useful if speed is of the essence – for example, you know the interviewers have seen all the candidates and plan to make up their minds quickly. On the other hand, e-mail can easily be ignored. If you have the luxury of time, then a letter is much more likely to make a lasting impression.

In your message, try to get across at least two or three of the following points:

✔ That you enjoyed the opportunity to meet the interviewer and to hear more about the organisation and the role.

✔ That you are very interested in the role, the challenge, the team, or the organisation.

✔ That you have the right attitude, skills, and experience for the job.

✔ That you would very much like a job offer or to be invited to the next stage of the interview process.

Figure 16-1 shows a sample letter to use as follow-up to your interview; don't copy it word for word, but take a look at what you *can* write.

A lot of people don't like to send follow-up letters to interviewers, saying that doing so is a bit cheesy or feels like begging for the job. But what do you have to lose? Nothing – because if you're unsuccessful you'll never see the interviewers ever again anyway. But think about what you may gain. Just possibly, your letter can land you that job.

Dear John,

I thought I would drop you a quick note to thank you for seeing me today. It was interesting to hear about the company's expansion plans. And I could tell that you obviously very much enjoy working there. The more I think about it, the more I would like to be a part of the company's future.

I hope that I managed to convey some of the qualities that would make me the right person for the job. I have nearly ten years' customer service experience in relevant sectors. In addition, I have the temperament and dedication to delivering high standard that would make me an excellent addition to your team.

I look forward to hearing from you soon - hopefully with the good news that you will be inviting me back for a second interview.

Yours sincerely,

Sarah Brown

Figure 16-1: Sending a follow-up after your interview may just tip the balance in your favour.

Ensuring Your References Are Positive

Many employers make job offers on the condition that your referees say positive things about you – or, at the very least, that they don't say anything hugely negative about you.

Before choosing people as referees, always ask their permission. Ideally, speak to them face-to-face so that you can gauge whether they are likely to make positive comments about you. If these people are reluctant, it may be that they didn't enjoy working with you and would feel uncomfortable commenting encouragingly about you!

If you parted on difficult terms with your last boss, you may not want to ask him or her for a reference. However, any organisation that is thinking of taking you on certainly wants a reference from your last employer. One (slightly sneaky) way round having to get a reference from your last boss is to ask another manager within the company to provide one. Perhaps you worked closely with the marketing manager or a director in another department and can ask one of them to write a complimentary reference for you. However, if a potential employer asks for a reference from your last boss, you may need to come clean.

Evaluating the Experience

Whether successful in being offered a job or not, always take the opportunity to think about what you did during an interview. How effective were you? And what can you do differently next time?

Rating your own performance

Take a few minutes to think about how well or badly the interview went. You really do benefit from taking the time to sit down and think about the lessons to take on board for future interviews.

Make notes straight after your interview (see the section 'Taking Notes after the Interview' earlier in this chapter) to ensure you don't forget any of the details. If you can, write down your impressions as soon as you get home after an interview when all the questions and your responses are fresh in your mind.

The best time to evaluate your performance really is the moment you get home. If you wait until you hear from the interviewers, the details of the interview may be too blurred by the passing of days or weeks for you to be able to review your performance with any accuracy. Begin your self-evaluation by jotting down some notes in answer to the following questions:

- ✔ What went well? What were you pleased with?

- ✔ What did you find difficult about the interview?

- ✔ What will you do differently in future interviews?

If you were unsuccessful in getting the job, take heart from the fact that even the very best candidates get knocked back sometimes. Don't let rejection get you down. The important thing is to calmly evaluate what you did well and what you can do better next time.

If you want to be more diligent in evaluating your own performance, think through some of these specific areas:

- ✔ **Research:** How would you rate your fact-finding on the company? Did the interviewers expose any areas of your research (or lack of it)? Reading Chapters 2 and 9 will help in advance of your next interview.

- ✔ **Interviewers' questions:** Were there any particular questions that you could have answered better? Check the relevant chapters of this book to work out a better answer for next time.

- ✔ **Rapport:** Did you smile and demonstrate your enthusiasm throughout the interview? Did you succeed in warming up the interviewers? If not, what can you do differently next time? (Refer to Chapter 3 for tips on creating rapport.)

✔ **Your questions:** What questions did you ask? And what questions should you have asked to demonstrate your knowledge and enthusiasm for the company? (See Chapter 15 for help constructing great questions.)

✔ **Dress code:** Were you dressed in a style similar to the interviewers? (Refer to Chapter 2 for further advice on getting your look right.)

Finding out what went wrong

If you're unsuccessful, try to get feedback from the interviewers as to what you could have done differently. If possible, arrange a time to call the interviewers to get their candid opinions.

Unfortunately, interviewers hate giving negative feedback. When they do give honest feedback, they often say that candidates get argumentative. So most interviewers have decided giving constructive feedback to unsuccessful candidates isn't worth the bother. Choose your words carefully in order to encourage the interviewers to be as candid as possible.

 Explain to the interviewers that some honest feedback would be invaluable in helping you to perform better in future interviews. Assure them that you won't try to change their minds. Be polite, but do persevere!

 Don't let the interviewers fob you off by saying *I'm afraid there was simply another candidate with better skills and experience.* This line is a common get-out clause that interviewers use to avoid giving any more incisive feedback!

If given the opportunity, ask the interviewers questions such as:

✔ *How do you think I came across? Was there anything I did or said that in the slightest way may have put you off me?*

✔ *Did you have any concerns about my experience or skills?*

✔ *Were there any questions that you felt I didn't answer to your satisfaction?*

✔ *If you don't mind me asking, what was it that the successful candidate said or did that helped them get the job?*

When the interviewers tell you their views, never argue with them or try to change their minds. Simply listen and scribble down some notes to capture their feedback. Whether or not you agree with the interviewers, they are entitled to their views. Finally, always thank them for their time, and then end the phone call politely.

Don't just ignore the interviewers' feedback. If they had a negative view on either your skills or how you came across, then other interviewers can easily feel the same way. Do something about it!

Knowing when to call if you don't hear anything

Interviewers often say that they'll get back to you – either by phone or in writing – 'within a few days' and then fail to do so. Of course, you'll be waiting on tenterhooks – so when is it okay to give them a call?

In general, wait twice as long as the interviewers said that they would take before getting in touch. Try to speak directly to one of the interviewers, reintroduce yourself and explain that you were wondering whether they have made a decision yet. Maintain a polite and professional tone (refer to Chapter 14 for further advice on how to conduct yourself over the phone), as you don't want to put the interviewer off if he or she has yet to make a decision.

Never imply that you need to find out because you have received another job offer unless this is true – the interviewer can call your bluff!

Part V
The Part of Tens

"It says on your CV, your one fault is that you tend to get disheartened when things look as if they're going wrong."

In this part . . .

The Part of Tens contains two useful chapters. I start with a cautionary list of the biggest interviewing pitfalls. I've interviewed hundreds of people and watched countless other interviews – and I don't want you to fall into one of these classic interviewing traps.

In the second chapter within this part, I suggest tips for building your long-term career. A career consists of more than simply moving from one job to another. And in this chapter I take you through some of the best advice for pursuing a fulfilling and successful long-term career.

Chapter 17

Ten Cardinal Sins of Interviewing

*P*reparing good answers to typical questions provides you with a great foundation to put in a cracking interview performance. But many candidates go wrong by committing some cardinal sins of interviewing. In this chapter, I share with you the most common mistakes that candidates make. Be sure that none of these happen to you!

Turning Up Late

Getting to an interview late is a huge no-no! The interviewers may have a packed schedule of interviews for the day, and a late arrival almost certainly makes them feel annoyed with you before you've even met.

Always carefully plan your journey to the interview. Make sure that you know the route to take whether driving or using public transport. And plan in plenty of time for contingencies – what if you encounter road works or one particular train gets cancelled?

Add at least 50 per cent more time to your journey than you think you need. If you arrive early, you can always find a nearby cafe to while away the time. Take a paper with you and catch up on what's happening in the world in case the interviewers want to make chitchat about the news. Some people like to go over their CVs one more time, but I'd recommend that now is too little too late – you really should have done all your preparation well before now!

If you're running late, call ahead to give the interviewers as much advance warning as possible.

Getting the Dress Code Wrong

Turning up to an interview and realising that you're dressed inappropriately makes you feel incredibly foolish. Yes, the organisation may have a casual dress code, but many interviewers make the effort to dress more smartly for interviews as they see themselves as official representatives of their organisation.

Other organisations pride themselves on their casualness – for example many of the creative types in media, advertising, and fashion distinguish themselves from *the suits* (lawyers, accountants, and personnel types) partly by how they dress. And turning up in a smart suit makes you seem dull and undesirable in these people's eyes.

If in any doubt, always call ahead to ask about the dress code. Don't allow yourself to be fobbed off by a receptionist who probably won't know what the interviewers may be wearing for the interview. Speak to one of the interviewers – or at least one of their personal assistants.

Being Rude to Receptionists

I know of a few candidates who have ruined their chances by being a bit off-hand with a receptionist, secretary, or personal assistant. Interviewers often ask receptionists or their PAs what they thought of you and a slightly flippant gesture at someone or a dismissive comment can be fatal. And you can bet that any rudeness on your part gets taken into account by the interviewers.

You're being observed and evaluated from the moment you arrive at an employer's premises. Every single person from the organisation who interacts with you – or even sees you – can potentially feed information back to the interviewers.

Getting Off to a Shaky Start

First impressions count! If you appear nervous in your first few minutes, you make it much harder for yourself as you'll be fighting against the interviewers' initial impression of you.

Follow these tried-and-tested tips for making your first couple of minutes go smoothly:

1. Smile broadly as you enter the room.

2. Say hello and something like *It's good to meet you* or *Great to meet you* – and say it with enthusiasm.

3. Maintain eye contact while saying hello.

4. Give the interviewers a firm (but not vice-like) hand-shake; and then follow their lead by sitting down when they do.

Create the impression that you're an upbeat and optimistic person. Compliment the interviewers about their organisation or make a positive comment about anything that strikes you:

✔ *I'm terribly impressed by this building – I really like your reception area.*

✔ *It's great to be here. And, by the way, your receptionists are so friendly.*

✔ *This is such a good location for your offices – how long have you been based here?*

✔ *It's such a lovely day outside – almost a shame to have to be indoors. But it's good to be here.*

Make your comment genuine and say it sincerely!

Giving a Monologue

Lengthy answers are tedious. If you speak for too long, you'll bore the interviewers. Remember that you may be the sixth candidate the interviewers have seen today or the twentieth over the course of several days.

Interviewers have a short attention span. But, unfortunately, they are also often inept at interrupting candidates – even when those candidates may be boring them to death. So interviewers usually just sit there mutely, pretending to listen while secretly thinking about what they may have for dinner that evening.

Try to speak for no more than two minutes at a time. Even when the interviewers seem rapt, check with them halfway through a lengthy answer by asking: *Is this useful? Shall I go on?*

Interviewers are generally polite enough to maintain eye contact even if they are incredibly bored. But they often fail to nod when they're not interested. So watch out for this tell-tale sign and either speak more briefly or inject a bit more energy into your performance if no one's nodding.

Answering in Monosyllables

Nerves can get the better of some candidates and they dry up under the stress of being interviewed. Failing to give enough detail is another fatal mistake.

Avoid answering in monosyllables. Remember that even if the interviewers ask you a closed question, such as *Did you have a good journey?*, you should answer in a sentence or two. Don't just answer *No* or *Yes, thanks* – it makes the interviewers feel as if speaking to you is like trying to get blood out of a stone.

Speak for a couple of sentences for every question that you're asked. For most questions – especially those asking you for examples of situations that you've been in – aim to speak for at least five or six sentences.

Failing the Luton Airport Test

I worked for a big management consultancy, and we applied a subtle test to interview candidates. Apart from trying to establish their leadership and teamworking skills, their intelligence and analytical abilities, we considered candidates in the light of the *Luton Airport Test*.

Imagine this scenario: You're stuck at Luton Airport with the candidate. Your flight has been cancelled and you have nothing to do but sit and wait. Would you be able to have an interesting conversation with the candidate? Or would you be tempted to throw yourself under the next plane?

Given two equally skilled and experienced candidates, the interviewers are going to plump for the one who is more interesting. So, put simply, the Luton Airport Test is an assessment of whether the interviewers like you and want to work with you.

Usurping the Balance of Power

One of the unspoken rules of interviews is that the interviewers are in control, and you must follow their lead. Break this fundamental rule at your peril.

No matter how strange an interviewer's question, try to answer it. Even if the interviewers ask you to talk about your childhood or tell them a joke, you must attempt to do your best.

Unless the question is illegal, don't ever say, *That's an odd question* or ask, *Why do you want to know that?* Even if the interviewers do ask you an illegal question, you may want to answer it anyway (see Chapter 13 for more advice on this).

Discussing Money Too Soon

Most of us work because we need to earn a living. Of course enjoying your job is also important, but the truth is that a lot of people wouldn't work if they could afford not to!

However, interviewers often see candidates asking about the pay and benefits too soon in the interview process as rather gauche. If you need to pass through several rounds of interviews, only talk about money in the final round.

The best time to talk about money is after you've been offered the job. Failing that scenario, only talk about money if the interviewers ask you about it first.

Having No Questions to Ask

If you say you have no questions for the interviewers, you send out the clear message that you are not overly interested in the job. And, if you aren't that interested, why will they offer you the position?

Always ask at least two or three questions. If you feel all your factual questions have been answered during the course of the interview, you can ask the interviewers why they enjoy working for the organisation.

Chapter 15 is packed with advice and suggestions on how to construct effective questions – so you really have no excuse to go blank!

Chapter 18

Ten Tips to Creating the Perfect Career

In This Chapter

▶ Understanding what matters for long-term career success

▶ Finding the right job for you

*I*mproving your interview technique helps you to nail a new job. But having a great career involves more than simply getting one new job after another – it requires a bit of fore-thought and planning. In this chapter, I guide you through my ten top tips for creating a fulfilling and rewarding lifelong career.

Knowing What You Want in a Job

Many people aren't that happy in their jobs. But given that we often spend more time at work than we do at home, wouldn't thinking about how we can be more fulfilled in our jobs make good sense? Only when you have an idea of where you want to go can you start to think about the steps necessary to get there.

So take a bit of time to think about what you would like to be doing in five or ten years' time. Will you be happy doing more of the same or something entirely different? Do you want a promotion?

Take some time to think about how you'd like your career remembered when you're gone. If you have any unrealised ambitions, what should you be doing differently in order to achieve them? What training or practical experience do you need to help you achieve your goals?

Understanding Yourself

Many people hold themselves back at work because they delude themselves about their true strengths and weaknesses. To some extent, I'd say that pretty much everybody allows themselves a few delusions. And often the reason people can't get a new job is because interviewers can see some weakness in them that they refuse to see in themselves.

You need to understand your weaknesses before you can work on them. And the best way of identifying these weaknesses is to gather feedback from people who know you. Identify six people who know you in a work context and send them an e-mail asking for their help. You may choose colleagues or ex-colleagues, clients or customers, suppliers, or even an ex-boss. Tell these people that you'll greatly value their candid opinions on your strengths and weaknesses in order to help you with your career development. Make it clear to them that you don't simply want compliments and platitudes, but some insight into how you come across to others. Simply ask these people three questions:

- ✔ *What are my strengths?*
- ✔ *What are my weaknesses?*
- ✔ *How can I improve on my weaknesses?*

Think carefully about the right people to ask to help you. Avoid choosing friends or family who don't know how you behave at work. Also, friends and family may not feel comfortable giving you incisive feedback for fear of offending or upsetting you.

Working on Your Weaknesses

Don't ignore the feedback you receive from people (see the preceding section, 'Understanding Yourself'). Dismissing feedback and thinking that these people don't understand the real you is easy. But remember that if the people who know you can see certain weaknesses in you, then employers may decide not to give you a job because they can see those weaknesses too.

Candidates are becoming increasingly sophisticated in how they present themselves at interviews. Competition is increasingly tougher for the best jobs too, so take every opportunity to work on your weaknesses.

Ask people for help in tackling your weaknesses. Trusted colleagues, your manager, or even friends may have some ideas for how to make you more effective at work. Do you perhaps need training in a particular skill? Or do you just need to behave in a different fashion – perhaps being more assertive, sympathetic, or tactful? Ask the people that you trust – and then listen to them.

Networking Widely

A massive market of jobs is never advertised, but instead filled by word-of-mouth alone. And the only way to access those jobs is to make sure that people know about you, your skills, and experience. If you only take on board one piece of advice for building a successful and rewarding career – network more widely.

Get out of your office more often. Go to conferences and exhibitions for people in your field. Look for opportunities to meet new people and let them know about who you are and what you can do. You never know when someone may know someone who is looking to fill a vacancy with a person just like you.

When you do meet people, show a genuine interest in them rather than trying to sell yourself to them. Ask them about their jobs, what they enjoy, and what frustrates them. Try to be a good listener – this wins you more friends than trying to be a good talker.

Meeting new people is easy. But the hard work comes in keeping in touch with them and making sure that they remember you when someone they know is looking for a job. Drop people an e-mail every few months to see how they are.

Continue to demonstrate your genuine interest in them rather than simply talk about yourself; this keeps you at the forefront of their minds.

Asking to See Offers in Writing

Being offered a job is a great feeling. Hurrah and congratulations! But always ask to see an offer in writing. You can read through the document at your own pace and see exactly what the company is offering you. Apart from the salary itself, does the offer satisfy your needs in terms of benefits?

Think about perks such as:

- ✔ Medical insurance, death-in-service benefit.
- ✔ Bonuses contingent on individual, team, or company performance.
- ✔ Pension contributions.
- ✔ Car or car allowance.
- ✔ Use of a mobile phone and/or laptop computer.

Employers can and do occasionally retract offers due to unforeseen circumstances. So keep attending interviews and never close off other job options until you've signed an iron-clad employment contract.

Evaluating the Job Thoroughly

Apart from the pay and benefits, other factors are also important in considering a job offer. How much do you really want this job? How does it fit in with your long-term career plans? Given that you may be spending many months or even years in the job, do you think you'll enjoy it?

No employer is ever perfect for you. Always ask for at least a couple of days – more if the role is senior – to think about a job offer and consider whether the position is totally right for you.

Think through some of the following considerations in weighing up whether to accept a job:

- ✔ **Usage of skills:** Will this job allow you to use your favourite skills most (or at least some) of the time? For example, if you enjoy face-to-face contact with customers, will you be able to do so or will you be mostly dealing with paperwork or spending time in meetings with colleagues?

- ✔ **Advancement opportunities:** Does this job fit into your long-term career plans? Are you looking to accept this offer because you think you will enjoy the position? Or are you looking to use this job as a stepping-stone for a future job – either within or outside of the company?

- ✔ **Your boss:** Can you meet your boss first? Or have you already met him or her? To what extent do you think you will get on with them and agree with their style of management?

- ✔ **The people:** What are the rest of the team like? Are they the kind of people that you can work with? Can you imagine socialising with them?

- ✔ **The journey:** How long will you have to spend commuting to the company's offices? Is it an easy commute or a complicated journey? Would you have to relocate or would you be able to negotiate working from home occasionally to offset a long journey?

- ✔ **Work environment:** How much do you like the actual workspace and building in which you'll be working? And to what extent do you like the local area around the building or the town the organisation is based in?

Considering Culture Carefully

Being chosen over other candidates and offered a new job is thrilling. But remember that employers rarely tell candidates exactly what working for their company is like – or at least not voluntarily. Interviewers and recruitment brochures are there to sell a job to prospective candidates.

In deciding whether to accept a new job offer, you should weigh up the *culture* of the organisation – the unspoken rules that govern how people really behave at work.

Talking to people who already work there is the best way to evaluate the organisation's culture. After you're offered the job, ask the interviewers whether you can meet – or at least have a telephone conversation with – some of the current members of the team. What do they enjoy about working for the company? What frustrates them? What is it really like to work for that company on a daily basis? People are usually guarded in talking to potential new colleagues, but with a little (polite) probing, you may find out some interesting information.

Make sure that you can satisfy yourself on cultural issues and questions. Consider the following questions:

- ✔ How do managers treat employees?
- ✔ To what extent does the company seem to communicate in an open and fair manner?
- ✔ Does the atmosphere seem sociable and friendly?
- ✔ Do you like the company's dress code?
- ✔ How much autonomy do employees seem to be given to do their work?

At the end of the day, can you satisfy yourself that you'll be happy trying to fit into the unspoken rules of how to behave in this new company?

If you have any niggling doubts about whether a job is right for you, then ask for more time to think about it. Never allow an employer to pressure you into accepting a position simply because they need someone to start quickly.

If you continue to have serious reservations about the suit-ability of an organisation, be willing to consider walking away from it. Turning down a job offer is far better than accepting it and quitting a few months down the line.

Negotiating a Good Deal for Yourself

Your best chance to negotiate a better deal for yourself is when the interviewers offer you the job. They have eliminated the other candidates and decided that you are the only person that they want. If you're unsatisfied with the salary or benefits, or perhaps the conditions of the job, you have nothing to lose by asking to have them tweaked to your satisfaction.

Don't think only about asking for more pay or benefits. You may also want to consider options such as:

- ✔ The hours that you work – for example, would you want to start earlier and finish earlier (or vice versa)?

- ✔ The nature of your job – perhaps you would like to alter your job description to add or remove certain duties, or change the manager you work for.

- ✔ The opportunities for training – you may want your employer to give you time off or financial sponsorship for a training course or qualification.

Whenever you want to ask for more, always try to justify what you're asking for. Don't just say *what* you want, but explain *why* it benefits both you and the employer. Emphasise what you bring to the company and what you intend to achieve for your employer.

When negotiating, bear in mind that a difference exists between what you *want* and what you *need*:

- ✔ **Wants:** What do you ideally want to get out of the negotiation? This may be a wish list of benefits that you may be looking to extract from an employer before agreeing to work for them. But bear in mind that you are unlikely to get everything that you ask for.

- ✔ **Needs:** What are your minimum needs? For example, you may *want* a £35,000 salary, but be prepared to accept £32,000 because it would meet your *need*. Understanding your wants versus your needs helps you to bear in mind your absolute bottom line and what compromises you may be willing to accept when negotiating for more.

Asking and demanding are worlds apart. Asking for more in a positive and professional way may get you what you want. Demanding more only gets an employer's back up.

Investing in Your Future

Most people are full of enthusiasm on joining a new organisation. But that enthusiasm can fade after a few years or even months. And then those people end up putting themselves on autopilot – going through the motions but not thinking about what they can do to push themselves and develop in their careers.

Cruising is fine until you look for a new job. Interviewers want to know about your achievements. Will you have anything worthwhile to talk about?

Make sure that you build up your CV by participating in big projects, volunteering to join committees, chasing promotions, or at least moving departments every couple of years. Always think about storing up achievements to put onto your CV and talk about in future interviews.

Your employer may *say* that they have your best interests at heart – but in reality the needs of the organisation always come above yours. If you don't look after your own career, no one else will!

Looking for Opportunities to Grow

Employers don't like to give big pay rises to long-standing employees. And getting more responsibility can be difficult if an organisation is happy to leave you where you are. Often, the only way to get more money or responsibility is to change employers. So always keep an eye on the jobs sections of newspapers and relevant Web sites.

Keep in touch with headhunters and recruitment consultants. Even if you're not currently thinking about changing jobs, update your CV and send it to them at least once a year so that you're on file for possible future opportunities.

Index

• *I* •

• J •

• K •

• L •

• U •

• V •

• W •

FOR DUMMIES®

Do Anything. Just Add Dummies

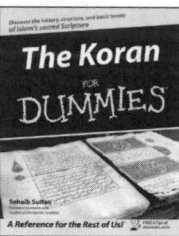